PERFECT PHRASES
in Spanish
for
HOUSEHOLD
MAINTENANCE
and CHILD CARE

**500+ Essential Words and Phrases
for Communicating with Spanish-Speakers**

Jean Yates

New York Chicago San Francisco Lisbon London Madrid Mexico City
Milan New Delhi San Juan Seoul Singapore Sydney Toronto

The **McGraw·Hill** Companies

Library of Congress Cataloging-in-Publication Data

Yates, Jean.
    Perfect Spanish phrases for household maintenance and child care / Jean Yates.
        p.   cm. — (Perfect phrases in Spanish)
    ISBN 0-07-149476-6 (alk. paper)
    1. Spanish language—Conversation and phrase books (for domestics)   I. Title.

    PC4120.S45Y38   2007
    468.3′42102464046—dc22   2007043628

1 2 3 4 5 6 7 8 9 10 11 12 13 14 15 16 17 18 19 20 21   DOC/DOC   0 9 8

ISBN 978-0-07-149476-2
MHID   0-07-149476-6

Contents

Contents

CHAPTER 2   ESTABLISHING BASIC POLICIES   33

CHAPTER 3   GENERAL CLEANING INSTRUCTIONS   45

Contents

Contents

CHAPTER 5   CHILD CARE   103

Acknowledgments

I would like to thank the following people for their thoughtful contributions to this book: Gloria Yates, my mother, who knows how to manage a household; Aura Obando and her daughter, Cindy, my dear friends, who know how to manage a household in Spanish; and Karen Young and Nancy Hall, my editors, who know how to make a manuscript into a book.

Introduction

In many parts of the United States, individuals and companies are employing at an increasing rate Spanish-speaking child care workers, housekeepers, and cleaning crews who do not speak English. This book is designed to provide such employers with simple phrases in Spanish that will enable them to communicate basic information to their employees, helping to ensure that they understand the information necessary for jobs to be done correctly, efficiently, and safely. In learning some Spanish phrases, employers often develop stronger working relationships with their employees, who are generally most appreciative of this interest.

It is very common for people who do not speak each others' languages to communicate with hand signals, gestures, or words they may have heard others say. This may lead to a certain level of mutual understanding, but it is certainly less than ideal, especially in a job setting, as it often ends in misunderstandings by both parties, can cause mishaps and bad feelings, and could even be dangerous. In this book, employers will find key words and phrases that will help them begin communicating with their Spanish-speaking housekeepers and child care professionals in a clear and correct manner right from the beginning. While this is not a course in grammar or conversation, those who consistently use these words and phrases with their employees will find that they are beginning to understand and use quite a bit of Spanish, and can actually build on this foundation to continue learning the language.

How This Book Is Organized

The phrases in this book are divided into five sections. In Chapter 1, you will find general words and expressions that are used every day to say such things as *hello* and *good-bye*, *please* and *thank you*, and convey other expressions of courtesy. Also in this section are the phrases that will enable you to both hire and terminate household help and to explain to an employee the general rules and policies of employment with you, including such topics as wages, social security payments, punctuality, and so forth. You will also find the words to help you express satisfaction or dissatisfaction with an employee's performance. In Chapter 2, you will find the phrases that involve establishing the basic policies that you set regarding working in your home. Chapter 3 includes expressions for introducing your home to a potential employee and giving general cleaning instructions that tell the way you would like things to be done. Chapter 4 provides specific expressions for the jobs normally done in each room of the house. Chapter 5 provides phrases relating to the care of children. The two glossaries of all the words used in the book are arranged in alphabetical order, the first from English to Spanish, and the second from Spanish to English. In addition, there is a table of the numbers from 0 to multiple millions, for handy reference.

Vocabulary Guidelines

Throughout the book there are phrases that allow for substitutable words. When this occurs, the word that can be replaced with another is <u>underlined</u>. Then one, two, or more words that could easily replace the underlined word are presented. This feature will help you memorize the most useful phrases, and generate an unlimited number of useful sentences. An example is shown in the following:

Please clean the stove.
    Por favor, limpie la estufa.
(por fah-BOR, LEEM-p'yeh lah ehs-TOO-fah)

the oven
    el horno
(ehl OR-noh)

the refrigerator
    la nevera
(lah neh-BEH-rah)

the floor
    el suelo
(ehl SWEH-loh)

Pronunciation Guidelines

Each phrase in Chapter 1 and Chapter 2 is printed in Spanish to the right of its equivalent English phrase, with a guide to its pronunciation written directly underneath. The symbols used are an approximation of how the words would sound if they were written in English, as illustrated below.

Vowels

To make a Spanish vowel sound, open your mouth and place your lips in position, and do not move your lips until you make the next sound.

Spanish Spelling	Approximate Pronunciation
a	ah
e	eh
i	ee
o	oh
u	oo

To make a vowel combination, begin with the first vowel, then move your lips into the position of the second.

ai	eye
ei	ay (like the *ei* in *weight*)
oi	oy
ui	wee
ia	yah
ie	yeh
io	yoh
iu	yoo
au	ah'oo
eu	eh'oo
ua	wah
ue	weh
uo	woh

Consonants

b	b
ca / co / cu	kah / koh / koo
ce / ci	seh / see
d (to begin a word)	d
d (after a vowel)	th (as in *brother*)
f	f
ga / go / gu	gah / goh / goo
ge / gi	heh / hee
h	silent (like the *h* in *honest*)
j	h
la / le / li / lo / lu	lah / leh / lee / loh / loo

al / el / il / ol / ul	adl / edl / eedl / odl / udl
ll	y / j
m	m
n	n
n (before c / g)	ng (like the *ng* in *finger*)
ña / ñe / ñi / ño / ñu	n'yah / n'yeh / n'yee / n'yoh / n'yoo
p	p
que / qui	keh / kee
r (at the beginning)	rrr (trilled)
r (between vowels)	d / tt / dd
bari	body
beri	Betty
biri	beady
ora	oughtta
vuru	voodoo
rr	rrr (trilled)
s	s
t	t
v	b
x	ks
y	y / j
z	s

Syllables

As a general rule, in the transcription each syllable that is printed in lower case letters should be pronounced with the same tone and length, and the syllable printed in capital letters should be emphasized, by saying it a little louder and longer than the others. For example, the word **bueno**, which means *good*, is represented as follows:

good   **bueno**
                                        (B'WEH-noh)

How to Get the Most Out of This Book

There are many ways that you can help build your Spanish
vocabulary:

- Use the pronunciation guidelines provided, but also listen to
  your employees and try to copy their pronunciation.
- Customize your phrases by substituting words with other words
  from the lists provided, and also with new words you may learn
  from your employee. Words that are underlined can be sub-
  stituted with words from the alphabetical lists provided in the
  glossaries.
- Keep a notebook—ask your employee to say or write down
  problematical words or expressions; then, if you cannot find
  the word in this book, seek help from a dictionary or a bilingual
  speaker.
- To learn new words from your employee, begin right away by
  memorizing the following question:

How do you say _____   **¿Cómo se dice _____ en español?**
   in Spanish?   (KOH-moh seh DEE-seh _____ ehn
                                eh-spahn-YOHL)

The words you get as answers to your question can be added to your
notebook to help you remember them.

Cultural Guidelines

In most Spanish-speaking countries, there are three ways to say *you*: **tú**, to a person you generally socialize with; **usted**, to any other person, including a person you work for or who works for you, and **ustedes**, to two or more people whom you are talking to at the same time. The phrases in this book are given in the **usted** form, and instructions are also provided for changing these to the plural **ustedes** form. This will ensure that you are speaking to your employees in a respectful manner that will certainly be appreciated. Employees will also respond to you with this form.

Some Hispanic cultures have a more relaxed concept of time than that generally accepted in the United States. You will need to make it clear that arriving on time and on the agreed day(s), especially for work, is very important here, and that if an emergency arises that causes an employee to be late or unable to work, you expect to be informed right away.

You may want to have some idea about the family situations of your employees, as family is generally very important in Hispanic culture. Your workers may be supporting a number of family members both here and back home. Be sure to make clear to those who work for you what your policies are for time off for family emergencies and celebrations as well as for personal illness. You may also wish to state right from the beginning your feelings about family members accompanying or visiting your employee while on the job. It may not seem unusual to a worker to bring her children with her to your home when they are not in school, for example, but you may not want to start such a practice. It is much better to state this at the beginning than to wait until it happens.

Chapter 1

Spanish Basics

Exchanging pleasantries and greetings with your Spanish-speaking employees is a great way to begin to build a stronger working relationship.

Greetings

Following are the most common ways to greet people and to say good-bye to them.

Hello.	**Hola.**
	(OH-lah)
Good morning.	**Buenos días.**
	(B'WEH-nohs DEE-ahs)
Good afternoon.	**Buenas tardes.**
	(B'WEH-nahs TAHR-thess)
Good evening.	**Buenas noches.**
	(B'WEH-nahs NOH-chess)
Good night.	**Buenas noches.**
	(B'WEH-nahs NOH-chess)

Good-bye.	**Adiós.**
	(ah-TH'YOHS)
See you later.	**Hasta luego.**
	(AH-stahl WEH-goh)
Have a nice day.	**Que le vaya bien.** (*lit*: May all go well for you—to someone who is leaving.)
	(keh leh BAH-yah B'YEN)

In Spanish sometimes you need to change your greeting, depending on whether you are speaking to a male or female and also when you speak to several people together. In the examples below, you'll see four ways to say "Welcome":

Welcome. (to a male)	**Bienvenido.**
	(b'yen-beh-NEE-thoh)
Welcome. (to a female)	**Bienvenida.**
	(b'yen-beh-NEE-thah)
Welcome. (to an all-male or mixed group)	**Bienvenidos.**
	(b'yen-beh-NEE-thohs)
Welcome. (to an all-female group)	**Bienvenidas.**
	(b'yen-beh-NEE-thahs)

Pleasantries

Just like "Hi, how are you?" is usually the first thing we say to each other in English, its equivalent in Spanish is the most usual greeting.

How are you?	**¿Cómo está?**
	(KOHM-weh-STAH)

2

To say the same thing to more than one person, just add **n** to **está**, making **están**:

How are you (all)? **¿Cómo están?**
(KOHM-weh-STAHN)

Here are some stock answers:

Fine, thank you. **Bien, gracias.**
(B'YEN, GRAHS-yahs)

So-so. **Regular.**
(reh-goo-LAHR)
Más o menos. (lit: more or less)
(MAHS oh MEH-nos)

Not well. **Mal.**
(MAHL)

Family and Friends

"Family first" is an important concept in Hispanic culture, and asking about the health of family members is one way of showing that you understand and appreciate this.

Use the following formula to ask about one person:

How is your <u>mother</u>? **¿Cómo está su <u>mamá</u>?**
(KOHM-weh-STAH soo mah-MAH)

Just substitute any of the following words to ask about others:

father **papá**
(pah-PAH)

husband	**esposo**
	(eh-SPOH-soh)
wife	**esposa**
	(eh-SPOH-sah)
sister	**hermana**
	(ehr-MAH-nah)
brother	**hermano**
	(ehr-MAH-noh)
son	**hijo**
	(EE-hoh)
daughter	**hija**
	(EE-hah)

To inquire about more than one person at a time, just add **s** to **su**, to make the word plural, and add **n** to **está** (**están**):

How are your <u>parents</u>?	**¿Cómo están sus <u>papás</u>?**
	(KOHM-weh-STAHN soos pah-PAHS)
children	**hijos**
	(EE-hohs)
daughters	**hijas**
	(EE-hahs)
sisters and brothers	**hermanos**
	(ehr-MAH-nohs)
sisters	**hermanas**
	(ehr-MAH-nahs)

While we're on the subject of people important to us, let's include a few more whom we can't do without:

friend (male)	**amigo** (ah-MEE-goh)
friend (female)	**amiga** (ah-MEE-gah)
boyfriend	**novio** (NOH-b'yoh)
girlfriend	**novia** (NOH-b'yah)
boss (male)	**patrón /jefe** (pah-TROHN) / (HEH-feh)
boss (female)	**patrona / jefa** (pah-TROH-nah) / (HEH-fah)
neighbor (male)	**vecino** (beh-SEE-noh)
neighbor (female)	**vecina** (beh-SEE-nah)

These can also be made plural, by adding **s** (or **es** in the case of **patrón**). (It's probably not a good idea to make **novio** or **novia** plural.)

The "Magic" Words

These are the essential words for showing courtesy and respect. Memorize these right away.

Please.	**Por favor.** (por fah-BOR)
Thank you.	**Gracias.** (GRAH-s'yahs)

You're welcome.	**De nada.**
	(deh NAH-thah)
Excuse me.	**Disculpe.**
	(dees-KOOL-peh)
I'm sorry.	**Lo siento.**
	(loh S'YEN-toh)

Telling Present Time and Using Numbers 1–12

In the following section, you will find phrases for asking and telling the time. The numbers from 1–12, which you will need for other purposes as well, are introduced here.

What time is it?	**¿Qué hora es?**
	(KEH OH-rah ess)

This question is answered for *one o'clock* by the phrase:

It's one o'clock.	**Es la una.**
	(ess lah OO-nah)

For all other hours, use the following phrase, inserting a number between two and twelve:

It's <u>two</u> o'clock.	**Son las <u>dos</u>.**
	(sohn lahs DOHS)
three	**tres**
	(TRESS)
four	**cuatro**
	(K'WAH-troh)

Spanish Basics

five	**cinco** (SEENG-koh)
six	**seis** (SACE) (rhymes with *face*)
seven	**siete** (S'YEH-teh)
eight	**ocho** (OH-choh)
nine	**nueve** (N'WEH-beh)
ten	**diez** (D'YESS)
eleven	**once** (OHN-seh)
twelve	**doce** (DOH-seh)

For times in between the hours, use the following expressions:

It's one-fifteen.	**Es la una y cuarto.** (ess lah OO-nah ee K'WAHR-toh)
It's two-thirty.	**Son las dos y media.** (sohn lahs DOHS ee MEH-th'yah)
It's three-forty-five.	**Son las tres y cuarenta y cinco.** (sohn lahs TRESS ee k'wah-REN-ta ee SEENG-koh)

You can express *noon* and *midnight* as follows:

It's twelve o'clock noon.	**Es mediodía.** (ess meh-th'yoh-DEE-ah)

It's midnight.

Es medianoche.

(ess meh-th'yah-NOH-cheh)

To indicate *morning*, add **de la mañana** to any hour:

It's ten A.M.

Son las diez de la mañana.

(sohn lahs D'YESS deh lah

mah-N'YAH-nah)

For *afternoon* or *evening*, add **de la tarde**:

It's four P.M.

Son las cuatro de la tarde.

(sohn lahs K'WAH-troh deh lah

TAHR-deh)

For *night*, add **de la noche**:

It's nine P.M.

Son las nueve de la noche.

(sohn lahs N'WEH-beh deh lah

NOH-cheh)

Indicating Work Hours

When you want someone to be somewhere or to do something at a particular time, use the following time expressions. Note that *one o'clock* is slightly different from the others.

at one o'clock

a la una

(ah lah OO-nah)

at two o'clock

a las dos

(ah lahs DOHS)

at four-thirty	**a las cuatro y media**
	(ah lahs K'WAH-troh ee MEH-th'yah)

The concept of time may be a little fuzzier in Hispanic culture than it is here. The following expressions will indicate that you mean "gringo" time, i.e., "on the dot." (And don't forget the "magic" **por favor**!)

Come tomorrow.	**Venga mañana.**
	(BENG-gah mah-N'YAH-nah)
Be here at seven.	**Esté aquí a las siete.**
	(eh-STEH ah-KEE ah lahs S'YEH-teh)
on the dot	**en punto**
	(en POON-toh)
Be on time.	**Sea puntual.**
	(SEH-ah poon-TWAHL)
Come early.	**Venga temprano.**
	(BENG-gah tem-PRAH-noh)
Don't be late.	**No venga tarde.**
	(NOH BENG-gah TAHR-deh)
You will be finished at five o'clock.	**Terminará a las cinco.**
	(tehr-mee-nah-RAH ah lahs SEENG-koh)

Talking to More than One Person at a Time

Just as before, to give instructions to a group of people, just add **-n** to the main word:

Come. (to one person)	**Venga.**
	(BENG-gah)

9

Come. (to two or more people)	**Vengan.**
	(BENG-gahn)
Be here. (to one person)	**Esté aquí.**
	(eh-STEH-ah-KEE)
Be here. (to two or more people)	**Estén aquí.**
	(eh-STEN-ah-KEE)

Days of the Week

If you look at a Spanish calendar, you will see that the extreme left-hand column shows Monday, rather than Sunday, as you may be accustomed to. Sunday is put in the extreme right-hand column, putting the weekend days together. Most workers expect a free day per week, not necessarily on a weekend. This day is often referred to by workers as **mi día** (*my day*).

What day is today?	**¿Qué día es hoy?**
	(KEH DEE-ah ess OY)
Today is <u>Monday</u>.	**Hoy es <u>lunes</u>.**
	(OY ess LOO-ness)
Tomorrow is <u>Tuesday</u>.	**Mañana es <u>martes</u>.**
	(mah-N'YAH-nah ess MAHR-tess)
Wednesday	**miércoles**
	(M'YEHR-koh-less)
Thursday	**jueves**
	(H'WEH-bess)
Friday	**viernes**
	(B'YEHR-ness)
Saturday	**sábado**
	(SAH-bah-thoh)

| Sunday | **domingo** |
| | (doh-MEENG-goh) |

To indicate a day in the future, add **el** before the name of the day:

| Be here on Monday. | **Esté aquí el lunes.** |
| | (eh-STEH ah-KEE el LOO-ness) |

To indicate *always on that day* add **los** before the name of the day:

Come on Mondays.	**Venga los lunes.**
	(BENG-gah lohs LOO-ness)
Come every day.	**Venga todos los días.**
	(BENG-gah TOH-thohs lohs DEE-ahs)
Don't come on Sundays.	**No venga los domingos.**
	(NOH BENG-gah lohs
	doh-MEENG-gohs)

Months of the Year and Using Numbers 1–31

Did you notice that the days of the week are not capitalized in Spanish? It's the same with the months. Also, when giving the date in abbreviated form, the day and the month are reversed compared to English. In other words, 3/9/07 in English would be March 9, 2007. In Spanish it is September 3, 2007. Let's look at how these dates are written and said.

| What's the date? | **¿Cuál es la fecha?** |
| | (K'WAHL ess lah FEH-chah) |

11

It's the first of January.	**Es el primero de enero.**
	(ess el pree-MEH-roh deh eh-NEH-roh)

After "the first" day, dates are given in cardinal numbers, as in "the 'two' of January," "the 'three' of January," and so forth. Following are examples using all of the months, and numbers up to thirty-one.

It's the <u>second</u> of <u>January</u>.	**Es el <u>dos</u> de <u>enero</u>.**
	(ess el DOHS deh-NEH-roh)
the third of February	**el tres de febrero**
	(el TRESS deh feh-BREH-roh)
the fourth of March	**el cuatro de marzo**
	(el K'WAH-troh deh MAHR-soh)
the fifth of April	**el cinco de abril**
	(el SEENG-koh deh ah-BREEL)
the sixth of May	**el seis de mayo**
	(el SACE deh MAH-yoh)
the seventh of June	**el siete de junio**
	(el S'YEH-teh deh HOON-yoh)
the eighth of July	**el ocho de julio**
	(el OH-choh deh HOOL-yoh)
the ninth of August	**el nueve de agosto**
	(el N'WEH-beh deh ah-GOH-stoh)
the tenth of September	**el diez de septiembre**
	(el D'YESS deh sep-T'YEM-breh)
the eleventh of October	**el once de octubre**
	(el OHN-seh deh ohk-TOO-breh)

the twelfth of November	**el doce de noviembre** (el DOH-seh deh noh-B'YEM-breh)
the thirteenth of December	**el trece de diciembre** (el TREH-seh deh dee-S'YEM-breh)
the fourteenth	**el catorce** (el kah-TOR-seh)
the fifteenth	**el quince** (el KEEN-seh)
the sixteenth	**el dieciséis** (el d'yes-ee-SACE)
the seventeenth	**el diecisiete** (el d'yes-ee-S'YEH-teh)
the eighteenth	**el dieciocho** (el d'yes-YOH-choh)
the nineteenth	**el diecinueve** (el d'yes-ee-N'WEH-beh)
the twentieth	**el veinte** (el BAYN-teh)
the twenty-first	**el veintiuno** (el bayn-T'YOO-noh)
the twenty-second	**el veintidós** (el bayn-tee-DOHS)
the twenty-third	**el veintitrés** (el bayn-tee-TRESS)
the twenty-fourth	**el veinticuatro** (el bayn-tee-K'WAH-troh)
the twenty-fifth	**el veinticinco** (el bayn-tee SEENG-koh)

the twenty-sixth	**el veintiséis**
	(el bayn-tee-SACE)
the twenty-seventh	**el veintisiete**
	(el bayn-tee-S'YEH-teh)
the twenty-eighth	**el veintiocho**
	(el bayn-T'YOH-choh)
the twenty-ninth	**el veintinueve**
	(el bayn-tee-N'WEH-beh)
the thirtieth	**el treinta**
	(el TRAYN-tah)
the thirty-first	**el treinta y uno**
	(el TRAYN-tah ee OO-noh)

Talking About the Weather

Sometimes talking about the weather is more than just a pleasantry
—it can affect the work of the day. Following are the most common
expressions.

How's the weather?	**¿Qué tiempo hace?**
	(KEH T'YEM-poh AH-seh)
It's fine.	**Hace buen tiempo.**
	(AH-seh B'WEHN T'YEM-poh)
It's hot.	**Hace calor.**
	(AH-seh kah-LOR)
It's cold.	**Hace frío.**
	(AH-seh FREE-oh)
It's raining.	**Está lloviendo.**
	(eh-STAH yoh-B'YEN-doh)

It's snowing.	**Está nevando.**
	(eh-STAH neh-BAHN-doh)
It's windy.	**Hace viento.**
	(AH-seh B'YEN-toh)
It's sunny.	**Hace sol.**
	(AH-seh SOHL)
It's cloudy.	**Está nublado.**
	(eh-STAH noo-BLAH-thoh)
There's a storm.	**Hay una tormenta.**
	(EYE oo-nah tor-MEN-tah)

Interviewing an Employee

These are the phrases for learning the most basic information about your prospective employees.

What's your name?	**¿Cuál es su nombre?**
	(K'WAHL ess soo NOHM-breh)
Where are you from?	**¿De dónde es?**
	(deh THOHN-deh ess)
Where do you live?	**¿Dónde vive?**
	(DOHN-deh BEE-beh)
How long have you been here?	**¿Hace cuánto que vive aquí?**
	(AH-seh K'WAHN-toh keh BEE-beh ah-KEE)
Where did you work before?	**¿Dónde trabajó antes?**
	(DOHN-deh trah-bah-HOH AHN-tess)
What kind of work did you do?	**¿Qué tipo de trabajo hizo?**
	(KEH TEE-poh deh trah-BAH-hoh EE-soh)

Do you have any experience cleaning houses?	**¿Tiene experiencia en limpiar casas?** (T'YEH-neh ek-spehr-YEN-s'yah en leem-P'YAHR-KAH-sahs)
Have you worked as a babysitter before?	**¿Ha trabajado como niñera alguna vez?** (ah trah-bah-HAH-thoh koh-moh nee-N'YEH-rah ahl-goo-nah BESS)

Asking for References

Notice that the question about contacting "her" is exactly the same in Spanish as the one about contacting "you," when you are speaking to a female. Likewise, the question about "him" is the same as the one about "you," when you are speaking to a male.

Can you give me a reference?	**¿Me puede dar una referencia?** (meh PWEH-theh dahr oo-nah reh-feh-REN-s'yah)
How can I contact her?	**¿Cómo la puedo contactar?** (KOH-moh lah PWEH-thoh kohn-tahk-TAHR)
How can I contact him?	**¿Cómo lo puedo contactar?** (KOH-moh loh PWEH-thoh kohn-tahk-TAHR)
How can I contact you? (to a female)	**¿Cómo la puedo contactar?** (KOH-moh lah PWEH-thoh kohn-tahk-TAHR)
How can I contact you? (to a male)	**¿Cómo lo puedo contactar?** (KOH-moh loh PWEH-thoh kohn-tahk-TAHR)

Hiring an Employee

Following are some basic phrases that will help you establish a relationship with a new employee.

You're hired. (to a female)	**Usted está contratada.**
	(oo-STED eh-STAH kohn-trah-TAH-thah)
You're hired. (to a male)	**Usted está contratado.**
	(oo-STED eh-STAH kohn-trah-TAH-thoh)
You're hired. (to two or more)	**Ustedes están contratados.**
	(oo-STEH-thehs eh-STAHN kohn-trah-TAH-thohs)

Scheduling

Following are phrases that will help you establish days and hours of work. To substitute different days and times, find the suitable words on the previous pages.

Can you come . . .	**¿Puede venir...**
	(PWEH-theh beh-NEER)
every day?	**todos los días?**
	(TOH-thohs lohs DEE-ahs?)
every week?	**cada semana?**
	(KAH-thah seh-MAH-nah)
from Monday through Friday?	**de lunes a viernes?**
	(deh LOO-ness ah B'YEHR-ness)

once a week?	**una vez a la semana?**
	(OO-nah BESS ah lah seh-MAH-nah)
on Mondays?	**los lunes?**
	(lohs LOO-ness)
twice a week?	**dos veces a la semana?**
	(DOHS BEH-sess ah lah seh-MAH-nah
once a month?	**una vez al mes?**
	(OO-nah BESS ahl MESS)
twice a month?	**dos veces al mes?**
	(DOHS BEH-sess ahl MESS)
four hours a day?	**cuatro horas al día?**
	(K'WAH-troh OH-rahs ahl DEE-ah)
thirty hours a week?	**treinta horas a la semana?**
	(TRAYN-tah OH-rahs ah lah seh-MAH-nah)

Discussing Salary and Using Numbers 40+

It's important to establish how you will pay your employee right at the beginning. Review the numbers between one and thirty-one on page 121. Higher numbers are introduced below.

Your wages will be . . .	**Su sueldo será...**
	(soo-SWELL-doh seh-RAH)
twenty dollars an hour.	**veinte dólares por hora.**
	(BAYN-teh DOH-lah-ress por OH-rah)

<u>forty</u> dollars for two hours.	**<u>cuarenta</u> dólares por <u>dos</u> horas.**
	(k'wah-REN-tah DOH-lah-ress por DOHS OH-rahs)
forty-five	**cuarenta y cinco**
	(k'wah-REN-tah ee SEENG-koh)
fifty	**cincuenta**
	(seeng-K'WEN-tah)
sixty	**sesenta**
	(seh-SEN-tah)
seventy	**setenta**
	(seh-TEN-tah)
eighty	**ochenta**
	(oh-CHEN-tah)
ninety	**noventa**
	(noh-BEN-tah)
one hundred	**cien**
	(S'YEN)
one hundred (and) fifty	**ciento cincuenta**
	(S'YEN-toh seeng-K'WEN-tah)
two hundred	**doscientos**
	(dohs-YEN-tohs)
three hundred	**trescientos**
	(tress-YEN-tohs)
four hundred	**cuatrocientos**
	(k'wah-troh-S'YEN-tohs)
five hundred	**quinientos**
	(keen-YEN-tohs)
six hundred	**seiscientos**
	(say-S'YEN-tohs)

seven hundred	**setecientos**
	(seh-teh-S'YEN-tohs)
eight hundred	**ochocientos**
	(oh-choh-S'YEN-tohs)
nine hundred	**novecientos**
	(noh-beh-S'YEN-tohs)
one thousand	**mil**
	(MEEL)
two thousand	**dos mil**
	(DOHS MEEL)

You may have noticed that the numbers sixteen to nineteen are each written as one word (**dieciséis**, **diecisiete**, etc.) even though their literal meaning is "ten and six," "ten and seven," etc. The same is true for the numbers twenty-one to twenty-nine: **veintiuno** ("twenty and one"), **veintidós** ("twenty and two"), etc. Beginning with the thirties, and up to ninety-nine, similar combinations are written as three words in Spanish:

thirty-one	**treinta y uno**
	(TRAYN-tah ee OO-noh)
forty-two	**cuarenta y dos**
	(k'wah-REN-tah ee DOHS)
fifty-three	**cincuenta y tres**
	(seeng-K'WEN-tah ee TRESS)
sixty-four	**sesenta y cuatro**
	(seh-SEN-tah ee K'WAH-troh)
seventy-five	**setenta y cinco**
	(seh-TEN-tah ee SEENG-koh)
eighty-six	**ochenta y seis**
	(oh-CHEN-tah ee SACE)

ninety-seven	**noventa y nueve**
	(noh-BEN-tah ee N'WEH-beh)

The conjunction **y** (*and*) is important in these combinations. In contrast, while we sometimes use *and* with hundreds in English, **y** is never used with hundreds in Spanish:

one hundred (and) ten	**ciento diez**
	(S'YEN-toh D'YESS)
four hundred (and) sixty	**cuatrocientos sesenta**
	(K'WAH-troh-S'YEN-tohs seh-SEN-tah)
five hundred (and) seventy-five	**quinientos setenta y cinco**
	(keen-YEN-tohs seh-TEN-tah ee
	SEENG-koh)

Rates of Payment

The following phrases tell how to express "per" a period of time.

per hour	**por hora**
	(por OH-rah)
per day	**por día**
	(por DEE-ah)
per week	**por semana**
	(por seh-MAH-nah)
per month	**por mes**
	(por MESS)
for the completed job	**por el trabajo completado**
	(por el trah-BAH-hoh
	kohm-pleh-TAH-thoh)

Discussing Pay Periods

Making this clear at the beginning will help avoid misunderstandings.

I'll pay you . . .	**Le pagaré...**
	(leh pah-gah-REH)
at the end of each day.	**al fin de cada día.**
	(ahl FEEN deh KAH-thah DEE-ah)
at the end of the week.	**al fin de la semana.**
	(ahl FEEN deh lah seh-MAH-nah)
when you finish the job.	**cuando termine el trabajo.**
	(K'WAHN-doh tehr-MEE-neh el trah-BAH-hoh)
by check.	**con cheque.**
	(kohn CHEH-keh)
in cash.	**en efectivo.**
	(en eh-fek-TEE-boh)
I cannot pay you . . .	**No le puedo pagar...**
	(NOH leh PWEH-thoh pah-GAHR)
in advance.	**por adelantado.**
	(por ah-theh-lahn-TAH-thoh)
before the job is finished.	**antes que se termine el trabajo.**
	(AHN-tehs keh seh tehr-MEE-neh-el trah-BAH-hoh)

Discussing Taxes

The phrases in this section will help you make it clear whether you wish to pay your employee's taxes or if you expect her to pay her own.

I will pay your Social Security taxes.	**Yo pagaré sus impuestos de Seguridad Social.** (YOH pah-gah-REH soos eem-PWEH-stohs deh seh-goo-ree-THAD soh-S'YAHL)
You must pay your own Social Security taxes.	**Usted debe pagar sus propios impuestos de Seguridad Social.** (oo-STED deh-beh pah-GAHR soos PROH-p'yohs eem-PWEH-stohs deh seh-goo-ree-THAD soh-S'YAHL)
You must pay your own income taxes.	**Usted debe pagar los impuestos por sus ingresos.** (oo-STED deh-beh pah-GAHR lohs eem-PWEH-stohs por soos een-GREH-sohs)
I will help you with the documents.	**Yo la ayudaré con los documentos.** (YOH lah ah-yoo-thah-REH kohn lohs doh-koo-MEN-tohs)
I cannot help you with the documents.	**No puedo ayudarla con los documentos.** (NOH PWEH-thoh ah-yoo-DAHR-lah kohn lohs doh-koo-MEN-tohs)

Showing Appreciation for Good Work

These are the phrases everyone likes to hear.

You did a good job.	**Ha hecho buen trabajo.**
	(ah EH-choh B'WEN trah-BAH-hoh)
You did a great job.	**Hizo el trabajo muy bien.**
	(EE-soh el trah-BAH-hoh M'WEE B'YEN)
You are punctual.	**Usted es muy puntual.**
	(oo-STED ess m'wee poon-TWAHL)
I'm happy with your work.	**Me gusta su trabajo.**
	(meh GOO-stah soo trah-BAH-hoh)
I'm raising your salary.	**Voy a aumentar su sueldo.**
	(boy ah ah'oo-men-TAHR soo SWELL-doh)
I am paying you extra today.	**Hoy le doy algo extra.**
	(OY leh doy ahl-goh EK-strah)

Clearing Up Confusion

Be sure to tell your employees what to do if they have a problem or an emergency situation.

Call me if you cannot come.	**Llámeme si no puede venir.**
	(YAH-meh-meh see noh PWEH-theh beh-NEER)
In an emergency, call me.	**Si hay una emergencia, llámeme.**
	(see EYE oo-nah eh-mehr-HEN-s'yah YAH-meh-meh)

My telephone number is 202-769-5416.	**Mi teléfono es dos cero dos, siete seis nueve, cinco cuatro uno seis.** (mee teh-LEH-foh-noh ess DOHS SEH-roh DOHS, S'YEH-teh SACE N'WEH-beh, SEENG-koh K'WAH-troh OO-noh SACE)
Tell me if you have a problem.	**Dígame si tiene algún problema.** (DEE-gah-meh see T'YEH-neh ahl-goon proh-BLEH-mah)
Tell me if you do not understand.	**Dígame si no entiende.** (DEE-gah-meh see NOH en-T'YEN-deh)

Terminating an Employee

These are the words nobody wants to say or hear, but sometimes they are necessary.

I no longer need you. (to a male)	**Ya no lo necesito.** (YAH noh loh neh-seh-SEE-toh)
I no longer need you. (to a female)	**Ya no la necesito.** (YAH noh lah neh-seh-SEE-toh)
You are fired. (to a male)	**Usted está despedido.** (oo-STED eh-STAH dess-peh-THEE-thoh)
You are fired. (to a female)	**Usted está despedida.** (oo-STED eh-STAH dess-peh-THEE-thah)
Because . . .	**Porque...** (POR-keh)

you didn't do the job well.	**no hizo bien el trabajo** (NOH EE-soh B'YEN el trah-BAH-hoh)
you didn't come when I expected you.	**no vino cuando yo la (lo) esperaba.** (NOH BEE-noh k'wahn-doh yoh lah [loh] eh-speh-RAH-bah)
you never came on time.	**nunca llegó a tiempo.** (NOONG-kah yeh-GOH ah T'YEM-poh)
you work too slowly.	**trabaja muy lento.** (trah-BAH-hah m'wee LEN-toh)
you don't have the necessary skills.	**no tiene las habilidades necesarias.** (NOH T'YEH-neh lahs ah-beel-ee-THAH-thess neh-seh-SAHR-yahs)
you didn't follow instructions.	**no siguió las instrucciones.** (NOH see-G'YOH lahs een-strook-S'YOH-ness)
you broke a lot of things.	**rompió muchas cosas.** (rohm-P'YOH MOO-chahs KOH-sahs)
you don't get along with my son.	**no se lleva bien con mi hijo.** (NOH seh YEH-bah B'YEN kohn mee EE-hoh.
you have a bad attitude.	**tiene mala actitud.** (T'YEH-neh MAH-lah ahk-tee-TOOD)

Basic Questions and Answers

In this section you will learn how to form *yes-or-no* questions as well as those that begin with question words like *who*, *where*, *when*, etc. Typical answers are also provided.

Yes-or-No *Questions*

A *yes-or-no* (**sí o no**) question in Spanish is made by pronouncing a statement as a question. Examples:

End a *statement* on the same tone you began on.

You have the money.	**Tiene el dinero.**
	(T'YEH-neh el dee-NEH-roh)

End a *question* on a tone higher than the one you began on.

Do you have the money?	**¿Tiene el dinero?**
	(T'YEH-neh el dee-NEH-roh)

It would be especially polite to include the person's name in answering this type of question.

Yes, Dolores.	**Sí, Dolores.**
	(SEE, doh-LOH-ress)
No, María.	**No, María.**
	(NOH, mah-REE-ah)
Maybe.	**Quizás.**
	(kee-SAHS)
It depends.	**Depende.**
	(deh-PEN-deh)

God willing!   **¡Ojalá!**

(oh-hah-LAH)

Information Questions

The following general questions and possible answers are included to help you request or provide information.

Who . . . ?	**¿Quién... ?**
	(K'YEN)
I	**yo**
	(YOH)
you	**usted**
	(oo-STED)
he	**él**
	(el)
she	**ella**
	(EH-yah)
we (in a mixed or all-male combination)	**nosotros**
	(noh-SOH-trohs)
we (when both or all are female)	**nosotras**
	(noh-SOH-trahs)
you (all)	**ustedes**
	(oos-TEH-thehs)
they	**ellos**
	(EH-yohs)
they	**ellas**
	(EH-yahs)
With whom?	**¿Con quién?**
	(kohn K'YEN)

with me	**conmigo**
	(kohn MEE-goh)
with <u>you</u>	**con <u>usted</u>**
	(kohn oo-STED)
him	**él**
	(el)
her	**ella**
	(EH-yah)
them	**ellos**
	(EH-yohs)
Whose is it?	**¿De quién es?**
	(deh K'YEN ess)
It's mine.	**Es mío.**
	(ess MEE-oh)
It's yours / his / hers / theirs.	**Es suyo.**
	(ess SOO-yoh)
What is it?	**¿Qué es?**
	(KEH ess)
It's <u>this</u>.	**Es <u>esto</u>.**
	(ess EH-stoh)
that	**eso**
	(EH-soh)
Where is it?	**¿Dónde está?**
	(DOHN-deh eh-STAH)
It's <u>here</u>.	**Está <u>aquí</u>.**
	(eh-STAH ah-KEE)
there	**ahí**
	(ah-EE)
over there	**allí**
	(ah-YEE)

Where are you going?	**¿Adónde va?**
	(ah THOHN-deh bah)
I'm going <u>home</u>.	**Voy <u>a casa</u>.**
	(BOY ah KAH-sah)
to the supermarket.	**al supermercado.**
	(ahl soo-pehr-mehr-KAH-thoh)
When?	**¿Cuándo?**
	(K'WAHN-doh)
now	**ahora**
	(ah-OH-rah)
later	**más tarde**
	(MAHS TAHR-deh)
soon	**pronto**
	(PROHN-toh)
always	**siempre**
	(S'YEM-preh)
never	**nunca**
	(NOONG-kah)
Until when?	**¿Hasta cuándo?**
	(ah-stah K'WAHN-doh)
until <u>Monday</u>	**hasta el <u>lunes</u>**
	(ah-stah el LOO-ness)
until <u>three</u> o'clock	**hasta las <u>tres</u>**
	(ah-stah lahs TRESS)
How?	**¿Cómo?**
	(KOH-moh)
like this / like that	**así**
	(ah-SEE)
For how long?	**¿Por cuánto tiempo?**
	(por K'WAHN-toh T'YEM-poh)

for <u>two hours</u>	**por dos horas**
	(por dohs OH-rahs)
a few minutes	**unos pocos minutos**
	(OO-nohs poh-kohs
	mee-NOO-tohs)
How many are there?	**¿Cuántos hay?**
	(K'WAHN-tohs EYE)
There is one.	**Hay uno.**
	(eye OO-noh)
There are a lot.	**Hay muchos.**
	(eye MOO-chohs)
a few	**unos pocos**
	(OO-nohs POH-kohs)
How much is it?	**¿Cuánto es?**
	(K'WAHN-toh ess)
It's twenty dollars.	**Son veinte dólares.**
	(SOHN BAYN-teh DOH-lah-ress)
It's a lot.	**Es mucho.**
	(ess MOO-choh)
only a little	**muy poco**
	(m'wee POH-koh)

Chapter 2

Establishing Basic Policies

I n this section you will find phrases that will help you tell a prospective employee about your home and family.

Introducing Your Home

Your employee will need to know who lives in your house, who is allowed to come in your house, and who isn't. It's also a good idea to introduce any pets you may have. To tailor these phrases to your particular situation, you can find appropriate vocabulary in Chapter 1.

I live here alone. (male)	**Vivo aquí solo.**
	(BEE-boh ah-KEE SOH-loh)
I live here alone. (female)	**Vivo aquí sola.**
	(BEE-boh ah-KEE SOH-lah)
I live here with my husband and three children.	**Vivo aquí con mi esposo y tres hijos.**
	(BEE-boh ah-KEE kohn mee eh-SPOH-soh ee TRESS EE-hohs)
I have a dog.	**Tengo un perro.**
	(TENG-goh oon PEHR-roh)

I have a cat. | **Tengo un gato.**
(TENG-goh oon GAH-toh)

Do not let the cat out. | **No deje que salga el gato.**
(NOH DEH-heh keh SAHL-gah el GAH-toh)

I will be here while you are cleaning. | **Estaré aquí mientras usted limpia.**
(eh-stah-REH ah-KEE M'YEN-trahs oo-STED LEEMP-yah)

I won't be here while you are cleaning. | **No estaré aquí mientras usted limpia.**
(NOH eh-stah-REH ah-KEE M'YEN-trahs oo-STED LEEMP-yah)

Do not answer the door when I am out. | **No conteste la puerta cuando yo no estoy.**
(NOH kohn-TEH-steh lah PWEHR-tah k'wahn-doh yoh noh eh-STOY)

Do not let a stranger in the house. | **No deje entrar a ningúna persona que no conozca.**
(NOH DEH-heh en-TRAHR ah neeng-GOO-nah pehr-SOH-nah keh noh koh-NOHS-kah)

Do not leave the door open. | **No deje abierta la puerta.**
(NOH DEH-heh ah-b'yehr-tah lah PWEHR-tah)

Do not answer the telephone. | **No conteste el teléfono.**
(NOH kohn-TEH-steh el teh-LEH-foh-noh)

I will return at five o'clock. | **Volveré a las cinco.**
(bohl-beh-REH ah lahs SEENG-koh)

Your Employee's Transportation

Here are some phrases that will help you give your employee some ideas about how to get to your home.

The nearest bus stop is on _____ street.

La parada de autobuses está en la calle _____.
(lah pah-RAH-thah deh ah'oo-toh-BOO-sess eh-STAH en lah KAH-yeh _____)

I will pick you up at the bus stop.

Yo la recogeré en la parada de autobuses.
(YOH lah reh-koh-heh-REH en lah pah-RAH-thah deh ah'oo-toh-BOO-sess)

metro station

la estación del metro
(lah eh-stah-S'YOHN del MEH-troh)

the train station

la estación de trenes
(lah eh-stah-S'YOHN-deh TREN-ess)

I cannot pick you up.

No puedo recogerla.
(NOH PWEH-thoh reh-koh-HEHR-lah)

I will take you home.

Yo la llevaré a su casa.
(YOH lah yeh-bah-REH ah soo KAH-sah)

I cannot take you home.

No puedo llevarla a su casa.
(NOH PWEH-thoh yeh-BAHR-lah ah soo KAH-sah)

You can park here.

Usted puede estacionarse aquí.

(oo-STED PWEH-theh eh-stah-s'yoh-NAHR-seh ah-KEE)

over there.

allí.

(ah-YEE)

in the driveway.

en la entrada.

(en lah en-TRAH-thah)

on the street.

en la calle.

(en lah KAH-yeh)

Entering and Leaving Your Home

The following phrases will help you make it clear how your employee will enter your home.

Knock on the front door when you arrive.

Toque a la puerta cuando llegue.

(TOH-keh ah lah PWEHR-tah K'WAHN-doh YEH-geh)

Ring the bell.

Toque el timbre.

(TOH-keh el TEEM-breh)

Come in with the key.

Entre con la llave.

(EN-treh kohn lah YAH-beh)

Here is the key to the front door.

Aquí tiene la llave para la puerta principal.

(ah-KEE T'YEH-neh lah YAH-beh PAH-rah lah PWEHR-tah preen-see-PAHL)

I'll leave the door unlocked for you.

Dejaré la puerta abierta para usted.

(deh-hah-REH lah PWEHR-tah ah-B'YEHR-tah pah-rah oo-STED)

My neighbor will open the door for you.	**Mi vecina le abrirá la puerta.** (mee beh-SEE-nah leh ah-bree-RAH lah PWEHR-tah)

These phrases will help you tell your employee what to do before leaving your home.

Lock the door when you leave.	**Cierre la puerta con llave cuando salga.** (S'YEHR-reh lah PWEHR-tah kohn YAH-beh k'wahn-doh SAHL-gah)
Open the window.	**Abra la ventana.** (AH-brah lah ben-TAH-nah)
Close . . .	**Cierre...** (S'YEHR-reh)
the door.	**la puerta.** (lah PWEHR-tah)
Turn on the light.	**Encienda la luz.** (en-S'YEN-dah lah LOOSE)
Turn off . . .	**Apague...** (ah-PAH-geh)
the alarm system.	**el sistema de seguridad** (el see-STEH-mah deh seh-goo-ree-THAD)

Paying Your Employee

Following are phrases for explaining different options for paying your employee.

Here is your check.	**Aquí tiene su cheque.** (ah-KEE T'YEH-neh soo CHEH-keh)

I will leave your check on the kitchen table.	**Dejaré su cheque en la mesa de la cocina.** (deh-hah-REH soo CHEH-keh en lah MEH-sah deh lah koh-SEE-nah)
Here is your payment in cash.	**Aquí tiene su pago en efectivo.** (ah-KEE T'YEH-neh soo PAH-goh en eh-fek-TEE-boh)

Emergencies

Be sure to let your employee know how to contact you or someone else in case of an emergency, or to ask a question.

If you need me . . .	**Si me necesita...** (see meh neh-seh-SEE-tah)
call this number.	**llame este número.** (YAH-meh EH-steh NOO-meh-roh)
If you cannot reach me . . .	**Si no me alcanza...** (see noh meh ahl-KAHN-sah)
call my neighbor.	**llame a mi vecina.** (YAH-meh ah mee beh-SEE-nah)
Her / His number is . . .	**Su número es...** (soo NOO-meh-roh ess)
In an emergency, call 911.	**Si hay una emergencia, llame al 911.** (see eye oo-nah eh-mehr-HEN-s'yah YAH-meh ahl N'WEH-beh OO-noh OO-noh)

If you are sick, you should stay home.

Si usted está enferma, debe quedarse en casa.

(see oo-STED eh-STAH en-FEHR-mah deh-beh keh-THAHR-seh en KAH-sah)

Meals

Here are some phrases that will help you tell your employee what to do at mealtimes.

I will provide your lunch.

Yo proporcionaré su almuerzo.

(YOH proh-por-s'yoh-nah-REH soo ahl-MWEHR-soh)

your breakfast — **su desayuno** (soo deh-sah-YOO-noh)

your dinner — **su cena** (soo SEH-nah)

snacks — **comida liviana** (koh-MEE-thah lee-B'YAH-nah)

soft drinks — **refrescos** (reh-FRESS-kohs)

juice — **jugo** (HOO-goh)

milk — **leche** (LEH-cheh)

coffee — **café** (kah-FEH)

tea — **té** (TEH)

You may make your lunch here.

Usted puede hacer su almuerzo aquí.
(oo-STED PWEH-theh ah-SEHR soo ahl-MWEHR-soh ah-KEE)

You may eat . . .

Usted puede comer...
(oo-STED PWEH-theh koh-MEHR)

anything in the refrigerator.

lo que esté en la nevera.
(loh keh eh-STEH en lah neh-BEH-rah)

anything on this shelf.

lo que esté en esta repisa.
(loh keh eh-STEH en EH-stah reh-PEE-sah)

Please . . .

Por favor...
(por fah-BOR)

do not eat this.

no coma esto.
(NOH koh-mah EH-stoh)

bring your lunch.

traiga su almuerzo.
(TRY-gah soo ahl-MWEHR-soh)

do not cook here.

no cocine aquí.
(NOH koh-SEE-neh ah-KEE)

Taking Breaks

An employee may want to take a shower or rest in your home before leaving. Here are some phrases that are helpful in outlining guidelines.

You may take a shower here.

Usted puede ducharse aquí.
(oo-STED PWEH-theh doo-CHAR-seh ah-KEE)

Establishing Basic Policies

Here are soap and towels.	**Aquí tiene jabón y toallas.**
	(ah-KEE T'YEH-neh hah-BOHN ee TWAH-yahs)
You must not take a shower here.	**No debe ducharse aquí.**
	(NOH DEH-beh doo-CHAHR-seh ah-KEE)
You should take a shower before you come.	**Usted debe ducharse antes de venir.**
	(oo-STED DEH-beh doo-CHAHR-seh AHN-tess deh beh-NEER)
You should take a break.	**Usted debe descansar.**
	(oo-STED DEH-beh dess-kahn-SAHR)
sit down for a few minutes.	**sentarse unos minutos.**
	(sen-TAHR-seh oo-nohs mee-NOO-tohs)
have a cup of coffee.	**tomarse un café.**
	(toh-MAHR-seh oon kah-FEH)
Please do not smoke in the house.	**Por favor no fume en la casa.**
	(por fah-BOR NOH FOO-meh en lah KAH-sah)
You may rest here before you leave.	**Usted puede descansar aquí antes de irse.**
	(oo-STED PWEH-theh dess-kahn-SAHR ah-KEE AHN-tess deh EER-seh)
You may not rest here before you leave.	**Usted no debe descansar aquí antes de irse.**
	(oo-STED NOH DEH-beh dess-kahn-SAHR ah-KEE AHN-tess deh EER-seh)

The Employee's Friends and Family

Your employee may want to bring her own children with her to your house. These phrases will help you communicate your preferences about visitors.

You may bring your children with you . . .	**Usted puede traer a sus niños consigo...** (oo-STED PWEH-theh trah-EHR ah soos NEEN-yohs kohn-SEE-goh)
in an emergency.	**si hay una emergencia** (see eye oo-nah eh-mehr-HEN-s'yah)
Your children may wait here for you for one hour.	**Sus hijos pueden esperarla aquí hasta una hora.** (soos EE-hohs PWEH-then eh-speh-RAHR-lah ah-KEE AH-stah OO-nah OH-rah)
Do not bring your children here.	**No traiga a sus niños a la casa.** (NOH TRY-gah ah soos NEEN-yohs ah lah KAH-sah)
Your friends must not visit you here.	**Sus amigos no deben visitarla aquí.** (soos ah-MEE-gohs NOH DEH-ben bee-see-TAHR-lah ah-KEE)
You may use the telephone for brief messages.	**Usted puede usar el teléfono para mensajes breves.** (oo-STED PWEH-theh oo-SAHR el teh-LEH-foh-noh pah-rah men-SAH-hehs BREH-behs)

Do not use the telephone.

No debe usar el teléfono.
(NOH DEH-beh oo-SAHR el
teh-LEH-foh-noh)

Use the telephone only in an
emergency.

**Use el teléfono sólo en caso de una
emergencia.**
(OO-seh el teh-LEH-foh-noh
SOH-loh en KAH-soh deh oo-nah
eh-mehr-HEN-s'yah)

Entertainment While Working

Many people like to watch television or listen to the radio while working. The following phrases will help you set guidelines.

You may watch TV here.

Usted puede ver televisión aquí.
(oo-STED PWEH-theh behr teh-leh-
bee-S'YOHN ah-KEE)

Do not watch TV here.

No debe ver televisión aquí.
(NOH DEH-beh behr teh-leh-bee-
S'YOHN ah-KEE)

You may listen to the radio here.

**Usted puede escuchar la radio
aquí.**
(oo-STED PWEH-theh-eh-skoo-
CHAHR lah RAH-th'yoh ah-KEE)

Do not listen to the radio.

No debe escuchar la radio aquí.
(NOH DEH-beh-eh-skoo-CHAHR lah
RAH-th'yoh ah-KEE)

Keep the volume low.

Mantenga bajo el volumen.
(mahn-TENG-gah BAH-hoh el
boh-LOO-men)

Equipment and Supplies

What equipment and supplies will you provide, and what do you expect your employee to bring? The following phrases will help you make this clear.

I will buy <u>the cleaning equipment</u>.	**Yo compraré <u>los aparatos para la limpieza.</u>** (YOH kohm-prah-REH lohs ah-pah-RAH-tohs pah-rah lah leemp-YEH-sah)
the cleaning supplies	**los limpiadores** (lohs leemp-yah-THOR-ess)
Please bring <u>your vacuum cleaner.</u>	**Por favor, traiga <u>su aspiradora.</u>** (por fah-BOR TRY-gah soo ah-spee-rah-THOR-ah)
your own cleaning supplies	**sus propios limpiadores** (soos PROH-p'yohs leemp-yah-THOR-ess)
rags	**los trapos** (lohs TRAH-pohs)

Chapter 3

General Cleaning Instructions

H ere is the basic vocabulary for introducing your household employee to the rooms in your house. Notice that all of the words in this list are preceded by the article *the*. In the first group below, this is expressed by **la** (to show that they are of feminine gender), and for those in the second group by **el** (to show that they are of masculine gender). Now, there is nothing "feminine" or "masculine" about these rooms: it is simply the *name* of the room that has a gender. It is best to think of the two words as a unit; that is, instead of just learning **cocina** for *kitchen*, think of it as **la cocina**.

Rooms in the House

the kitchen	**la cocina**
	(lah koh-SEE-nah)
the pantry	**la despensa**
	(lah deh-SPEN-sah)
the living room	**la sala**
	(lah SAH-lah)
the family room	**la sala familiar**
	(lah SAH-lah fah-meel-YAHR)

the library	**la biblioteca**
	(lah bee-bl'yoh-TEH-kah)
the closet	**la guardarropa**
	(lah gwahr-thahr-ROH-pah)
the laundry room	**la lavandería**
	(lah lah-bahn-deh-REE-yah)
the dining room	**el comedor**
	(el koh-meh-THOR)
the office	**el despacho**
	(el deh-SPAH-choh)
the study	**el estudio**
	(el eh-STOO-th'yoh)
the hall	**el pasillo**
	(el pah-SEE-yoh)
the bedroom	**el dormitorio**
	(el dor-mee-TOR-yoh)
the bathroom	**el baño**
	(el BAHN-yoh)
the nursery	**el cuarto de los niños**
	(el KWAHR-toh deh lohs NEEN-yohs)
the playroom	**la sala de recreo**
	(lah SAH-lah deh reh-KREH-oh)
the basement	**el sótano**
	(el SOH-tah-noh)
the attic	**el desván**
	(el dess-BAHN)
the garage	**el garaje**
	(el gah-RAH-heh)
the porch	**el porche**
	(el POR-cheh)

the patio	**el patio**
	(el PAH-t'yoh)

In Spanish, the words for *the* (**el** and **la**) are made plural when the words that follow them are plural. Here, names of rooms preceded by **el** are made plural by changing **el** to **los**, then adding **s** to the name of the room. Those preceded by **la** are made plural by changing **la** to **las**, and adding **s** to the name of the room. Some examples follow:

the bedroom	**el dormitorio**
	(el dor-mee-TOR-yoh)
the bedrooms	**los dormitorios**
	(lohs dor-mee-TOR-yohs)
the closet	**la guardarropa**
	(lah gwahr-dahr-ROH-pah)
the closets	**las guardarropas**
	(lahs gwahr-dahr-ROH-pahs)

Establishing Priorities

These phrases will help you tell your employee what you want done on a particular day.

Clean the whole house.	**Limpie la casa entera.**
	(LEEMP-'yeh lah KAH-sah en-TEH-rah)
Begin with the kitchen.	**Empiece con la cocina.**
	(em-P'YEH-seh kohn lah koh-SEE-nah)
The most important cleaning today is the bathroom.	**Lo más importante hoy es limpiar el baño.**
	(loh MAHS eem-por-TAHN-teh oy ess leemp-YAHR el BAHN-yoh)

47

This room needs a thorough cleaning.	**Hay que limpiar esta habitación a fondo.** (EYE keh leemp-YAHR EH-stah ah-bee-tah-S'YOHN ah FOHN-doh)
Just straighten this room today.	**Solamente arregle esta habitación hoy.** (soh-lah-men-teh ahr-REH-gleh EH-stah-bee-tah-S'YOHN OY)
Don't clean my son's bedroom today.	**No limpie el dormitorio de mi hijo hoy.** (NOH LEEMP-'yeh el dor-mee-TOR-yoh deh mee-EE-hoh oy)

Straightening the House

You may want to tell your employee to move certain things from one room to another, to throw away certain things, and to keep others. These phrases will help you communicate your wishes.

Keep this.	**Guarde esto.** (GWAHR-deh EH-stoh)
Put it here.	**Póngalo aquí.** (POHNG-gah-loh ah-KEE)
Don't put it there.	**No lo ponga ahí.** (NOH loh POHNG-gah ah-EE)
Throw it in the trash.	**Tírelo a la basura.** (TEE-reh-loh ah lah bah-SOO-rah)
Don't throw it in the trash.	**No lo tire a la basura.** (NOH loh TEE-reh ah lah bah-SOO-rah)

Put the trash in the trash can.	**Ponga la basura en el basurero.**
	POHNG-gah lah bah-SOO-rah en el
	bah-soo-REH-roh)
Take it upstairs.	**Llévelo arriba.**
	(YEH-beh-loh ahr-REE-bah)
downstairs	**abajo**
	(ah-BAH-hoh)

A simple **a** can mean *to*—as in *to another place*—in Spanish. When **a** precedes **el**, it is contracted to **al**. There is no contraction of **a la**.

to the garage	**al garaje**
	(ahl gah-RAH-heh)
to the living room	**a la sala**
	(ah lah SAH-lah)

Places to Put Things

You can indicate exactly where you want things to be put away with these phrases.

Please put it in the closet.	**Por favor, póngalo en la guardarropa.**
	(por fah-BOR, PONG-gah-loh en lah gwahr-thahr-ROH-pah)
on the shelf.	**en la repisa.**
	(en lah reh-PEE-sah)
in the drawer.	**en el cajón.**
	(en el kah-HOHN)
in the corner.	**en el rincón.**
	(en el reen-KOHN)

49

on the floor.	**en el suelo.** (en el SWEH-loh)
up there.	**arriba.** (ahr-REE-bah)
down there.	**abajo.** (ah-BAH-hoh)
next to the toaster.	**al lado del tostador.** (ahl LAH-thoh del tohs-tah-THOR)
under . . .	**debajo de...** (deh-BAH-hoh deh)
on top of . . .	**encima de** (en-SEE-mah deh)
in front of . . .	**delante de** (deh-LAHN-teh deh)
in back of . . .	**detrás de** (deh-TRAHS deh)
between the refrigerator and the stove.	**entre la nevera y la estufa.** (EN-treh lah neh-BEH-rah ee lah eh-STOO-fah)

Giving Instructions

These phrases will help you tell how you want things done.

Do it like this.	**Hágalo así.** (AH-gah-loh ah-SEE)
Don't do it like that.	**No lo haga así.** (NOH loh AH-gah ah-SEE)
Wash it.	**Lávelo.** (LAH-beh-loh)

Don't wash it.	**No lo lave.**
	(NOH loh LAH-beh)
by hand	**a mano**
	(ah MAH-noh)
Dry it.	**Séquelo.**
	(SEH-keh-loh)
Wipe it.	**Pásele un trapo.**
	(PAH-seh-leh oon TRAH-poh)
Scrub it.	**Friéguelo.**
	(FR'YEH-geh-loh)
Polish it.	**Sáquele brillo.**
	(SAH-keh-leh BREE-yoh)

What Not to Do

You probably have certain items that are valuable to you, and you don't want to risk their being broken. The following phrases will help you deal with this. As always, adding **por favor** and **gracias** to any phrase makes it more comfortable to express your desires.

This is very fragile.	**Esto es muy frágil.**
	(Eh-stoh ess m'wee FRAH-heel)
old	**antiguo**
	(ahn-TEE-gwoh)
valuable	**valioso**
	(bahl-YOH-soh)
important to me	**importante para mí**
	(eem-por-TAN-teh pah-rah MEE)
Do not touch this.	**No toque esto.**
	(NOH TOH-keh EH-stoh)

Be very careful with this.	**Tenga mucho cuidado con esto.** (TENG-gah MOO-choh kwee-THAH-thoh kohn EH-stoh)
Don't clean this with <u>water</u>.	**No limpie esto con <u>agua</u>.** (NOH LEEMP-yeh EH-stoh kohn AH-gwah)
chemicals	**productos químicas** (proh-THOOK-tohs KEE-mee-kahs)

Pests

You will want to know if your employee finds insects or other pests. Following are some ways to tell her what you would like her to do in such a case.

Tell me . . .	**Dígame...** (DEE-gah-meh)
if you see <u>ants</u>.	**si encuentra <u>hormigas</u>.** (see en-KWEN-trah or-MEE-gahs)
spiders.	**arañas.** (ah-RAHN-yahs)
insects.	**insectos.** (een-SEK-tohs)
bugs.	**bichos.** (BEE-chohs)
mice.	**ratones.** (rah-TOH-ness)

General Cleaning Instructions

rats.	**ratas.**
	(RAH-tahs)
snakes.	**culebras.**
	(koo-LEH-brahs)
any pests.	**cualquier animal extraño.**
	(kwahl-K'YEHR ah-nee-MAHL
	ek-STRAHN-yoh)
Use this insecticide, like this.	**Use esta insecticida, así.**
	(OO-seh EH-stah een-sek-tee-SEE-thah, ah-SEE)
this spray	**este espray**
	(EH-steh eh-SPRY)
this trap	**esta trampa**
	(EH-stah TRΛHM-pah)
Be careful with chemicals.	**Tenga cuidado con los productos químicas.**
	(TENG-gah kwee-THAH-thoh kohn lohs proh-THOOK-tohs KEE-mee-kahs)
Vacuum up the dead bugs.	**Pase la aspiradora por los bichos muertos.**
	(PAH-seh lah-ah-spee-rah-THOR-ah por lohs BEE-chohs MWEHR-tohs)
Sweep . . .	**Barra...**

Chapter 4

Specific Projects Around the House

In this chapter you will find more specific terms to address the different areas of the house and the types of care they require.

The Kitchen

The word for *kitchen* in Spanish is the same as the word for *cuisine* or *cooking*.

the kitchen	**la cocina**
	(lah koh-SEE-nah)

Kitchen Appliances and Equipment

These words will help you point out what you want to be cleaned.

Clean the <u>stove</u>.	**Limpie la <u>estufa</u>.**
	(LEEMP-yeh lah eh-STOO-fah)
Don't clean . . .	**No limpie...**
	(NOH LEEMP-yeh)

the oven	**el horno** (el OR-noh)
the stove burners	**los quemadores de la estufa** (lohs keh-mah-THOR-ess deh lah eh-STOO-fah)
the hood	**la campana extractora** (lah kahm-PAH-nah ek-strahk-TOR-ah)
the broiler	**el asador** (el ah-sah-THOR)
the refrigerator	**la nevera** (lah neh-BEH-rah)
the freezer	**el congelador** (el kohn-heh-lah-THOR)
the sink	**el fregadero** (el freh-gah-THEH-roh)
the drain	**el desagüe** (el dess-AH-gweh)
the faucet	**la llave** (lah YAH-beh)
the dishwasher	**el lavaplatos** (el lah-bah-PLAH-tohs)
the garbage disposer	**el triturador** (el tree-too-rah-THOR)
the cupboards	**los gabinetes** (lohs gah-bee-NEH-tess)
the countertop	**el mostrador** (el mohs-trah-THOR)
the floor	**el suelo** (el SWEH-loh)

the small appliances	**los aparatos pequeños** (lohs ah-pah-RAH-tohs peh-KEN-yohs)
this appliance	**este aparato** (EH-steh ah-pah-RAH-toh)
the microwave oven	**el microondas** (el mee-kroh-OHN-dahs)
the toaster	**el tostador** (el tohs-tah-THOR)
the mixer	**el batidor** (el bah-tee-THOR)
the blender	**la batidora** (lah bah-tee-THOR-ah)
the food processor	**el procesador de alimentos** (el proh-seh-sah-THOR deh ah-lee-MEN-tohs)
the grill	**la parrilla** (lah pahr-REE-yah)
the canisters	**las latas** (lahs LAH-tahs)
the pots and pans	**los trastes** (lohs TRAH-stehs)
the large pot	**la olla** (lah OY-yah)
the frying pan	**la sartén** (lah sahr-TEN)
the big one	**la grande** (lah GRAHN-deh)
the small one	**la pequeña** (lah peh-KEN-yah)

the utensils	**los utensilios**
	(lohs oo-ten-SEEL-yohs)
the silverware	**los cubiertos**
	(lohs koob-YEHR-tohs)
the spoon	**la cuchara**
	(lah koo-CHAH-rah)
the fork	**el tenedor**
	(el teh-neh-THOR)
the knife	**el cuchillo**
	(el koo-CHEE-yoh)
the dishes	**los platos**
	(lohs PLAH-tohs)
the china	**la vajilla**
	(lah bah-HEE-yah)
the glasses	**los vasos**
	(lohs BAH-sohs)
the crystal	**el cristal fino**
	(el krees-TAHL FEE-noh)
the candlesticks	**los candelabros**
	(lohs kahn-deh-LAH-brohs)

Giving Instructions

Remember that you can change any instruction to *Don't* by placing **No** before the action word.

Wash it.	**Lávelo.**
	(LAH-beh-loh)
Don't wash it.	**No lo lave.**
	(NOH loh LAH-beh)

Specific Projects Around the House

by hand	**a mano**
	(ah MAH-noh)
in the dishwasher	**en el lavaplatos**
	(en el lah-bah-PLAH-tohs)
Dry it.	**Séquelo.**
	(SEH-keh-loh)
Wipe it.	**Pásele un trapo.**
	(PAH-seh-leh oon TRAH-poh)
Scrub it.	**Friéguelo.**
	(FR'YEH-geh-loh)
Polish it.	**Sáquele brillo.**
	(SAH-keh-leh BREE-yoh)
Be careful with it.	**Tenga cuidado con eso.**
	(TENG-gah kwee-THAH thoh kohn EH-soh)

Cleaning Products and Equipment

Many cleaning products used in this country are different from those used in other places. These phrases will help you make clear what product you want to be used for each task. Be sure to show your employee the container of any special brand-name products you use.

Use . . .	**Use...**
	(OO-seh)
Don't use . . .	**No use...**
	(NOH OO-seh)
this product	**este producto**
	(EH-steh proh-THOOK-toh)

these products	**estos productos**
	(EH-stohs proh-THOOK-tohs)
wax	**cera**
	(SEH-rah)
soap	**jabón**
	(hah-BOHN)
dishwasher detergent	**detergente para el lavaplatos**
	(deh-tehr-HEN-teh pah-rah el
	lah-bah-PLAH-tohs)
bleach	**lejía**
	(leh-HEE-ah)
chlorine bleach	**cloro**
	(KLOH-roh)
ammonia	**amoníaco**
	(ah-moh-NEE-ah-koh)
vinegar	**vinagre**
	(bee-NAH-greh)
water	**agua**
	(AH-g'wah)
cold water	**agua fría**
	(AH-g'wah FREE-ah)
hot water	**agua caliente**
	(AH-g'wah kahl-YEN-teh)
boiling water	**agua hirviente**
	(AH-g'wah eer-B'YEN-teh)
CAUTION: Don't mix ammonia with chlorine bleach.	**OJO: No mezcle amoníaco con cloro.**
	(OH-hoh: noh MESS-kleh ah-moh-NEE-ah-koh kohn KLOH-roh)

The following phrases will help you explain which cleaning aids you would like used for different cleaning tasks.

paper towels	**las toallas de papel**
	(lahs TWAH-yahs deh pah-PELL)
dish towels	**las toallas de los trastes**
	(lahs TWAH-yahs deh lohs
	TRAH-stehs)
the rag	**el trapo**
	(el TRAH-poh)
the sponge	**la esponja**
	(lah eh-SPOHN-hah)
the broom	**la escoba**
	(lah eh-SKOH-bah)
the dustpan	**la pala**
	(lah PAH-lah)
the mop	**el trapeador**
	(el trah-peh-ah-THOR)
the bucket	**la cubeta**
	(lah koo-BEH-tah)
this	**esto**
	(EH-stoh)
that	**eso**
	(EH-soh)

The Garbage Disposer

If you still have the instructions or owner's manual for using your garbage disposer (or other appliances), see if they are also written in Spanish. It's a good idea to save these and show them to your employee. Following are some general instructions:

To operate the garbage disposer:	**Para operar el triturador:** (pah-rah oh-peh-RAHR el tree-too-rah-THOR)
Turn on the cold water.	**Abra la llave del agua fría.** (AH-brah lah YAH-beh del-ah-gwah FREE-ah)
Turn on the machine.	**Encienda la máquina.** (en-S'YEN-dah lah MAH-kee-nah)
Push the garbage down with <u>this</u>.	**Empuje los desperdicios con <u>esto</u>.** (em-POO-heh lohs dess-pehr-DEE-s'yohs kohn EH-stoh)
Put the eggshells in the garbage disposer.	**Ponga las cáscaras de los huevos en el triturador.** (PONG-gah lahs KAH-skah-rahs deh lohs WEH-bohs en el tree-too-rah-THOR)
Wait a few moments.	**Espere unos momentos.** (eh-SPEH-reh OO-nohs moh-MEN-tohs)
Turn off the machine.	**Apague la máquina.** (ah-PAH-geh lah MAH-kee-nah)
Turn off the water.	**Cierre la llave.** (S'YEHR-reh lah YAH-beh)

Following are some phrases to warn your employee what *not* to do.

Do not put your hands in the machine.	**No ponga las manos en la máquina.** (NOH POHNG-gah lahs MAH-nohs en lah MAH-kee-nah)

Do not run the disposer without water.

No use el triturador sin abrir la llave del agua fría.
(NOH OO-seh el tree-too-rah-THOR seen ah-BREER lah YAH-beh del ah-gwah FREE-ah)

Do not let food sit in the disposer.

No deje los desperdicios en la máquina.
(NOH DEH-heh lohs dess-pehr-DEE-s'yohs en lah MAH-kee-nah)

Do not pour cleaners in the disposer.

No eche limpiadores en el triturador.
(NOH EH-cheh leemp-yah-THOR-ess en el tree-too-rah-THOR)

Don't put rice in the garbage disposer.

No ponga arroz en el triturador.
(NOH POHNG-gah ahr-ROHS en el tree-too-rah-THOR)

grease

grasa
(GRAH-sah)

large amounts

cantidades grandes
(kahn-tee-THAH-thess GRAHN-dess)

artichokes

alcachofas
(ahl-kah-CHOH-fahs)

celery

apio
(AH-p'yoh)

cornhusks

mazorcas
(mah-SOR-kahs)

rhubarb

ruibarbo
(r'wee-BAHR-boh)

asparagus

espárragos
(eh-SPAHR-rah-gohs)

63

potatoes	**papas**
	(PAH-pahs)
peelings	**peladuras**
	(peh-lah-THOO-rahs)
pasta	**pasta**
	(PAH-stah)
toothpicks	**palillos**
	(pah-LEE-yohs)
bones	**huesos**
	(WEH-sohs)
nuts	**nueces**
	(N'WEH-sess)
seeds	**semillas**
	(seh-MEE-yahs)
other hard substances	**otros elementos duros**
	(OH-trahs eh-leh-MEN-tohs
	DOO-rohs)
If the machine makes an unusual noise, turn it off.	**Si la máquina hace un ruido extraño, apáguela.**
	(see lah MAH-kee-nah AH-seh oon R'WEE-thoh ek-STRAHN-yoh, ah-PAH-geh-lah)
Do not let spoons or other objects fall into drain.	**No deje que caigan las cucharas u otros objetos al desagüe.**
	(NOH DEH-heh keh KAH'ee-gahn lahs koo-CHAH-rahs oo OH-trohs ohb-HEH-tohs ahl dess-AH-gweh)

The Dishwasher

Again, find your machine's operating instructions and, if possible, show the Spanish version to your employee. Following are general instructions:

To operate the dishwasher:	**Para operar el lavaplatos:** (pah-rah oh-peh-RAHR el lah-bah-PLAH-tohs)
Rinse the dishes.	**Enjuague los platos.** (en-H'WAH-geh lohs PLAH-tohs)
Place the dishes like this.	**Coloque los platos así.** (koh-LOH-keh lohs PLAH-tohs ah-SEE)
the silverware	**los cubiertos** (lohs koo-B'YEHR-tohs)
the utensils	**los utensilios** (lohs oo-ten-SEEL-yohs)
Do not put too many dishes in the machine.	**No ponga demasiados platos en la máquina.** (NOH POHNG-gah deh-mah-S'YAH-thohs PLAH-tohs en lah MAH-kee-nah)
Do not put this in the dishwasher.	**No ponga esto en el lavaplatos.** (NOH POHNG-gah EH-stoh en el lah-bah-PLAH-tohs)
Put the plates in the dishwasher.	**Ponga los platos en el lavaplatos.** (POHNG-gah lohs PLAH-tohs en el lah-bah-PLAH-tohs)
Don't put these pans in the dishwasher.	**No ponga estos trastes en el lavaplatos.** (NOH POHNG-gah EH-stohs TRAH-stehs en el lah-bah-PLAH-tohs)

Put the dishwasher detergent here.	**Ponga el detergente aquí.** (POHNG-gah el deh-tehr-HEN-teh ah-KEE)
Close the machine like this.	**Cierre la máquina así.** (S'YEHR-reh lah MAH-kee-nah ah-SEE)
Push the "On" button.	**Apriete el botón « ON ».** (ah-PR'YEH-teh el boh-TOHN « ON »)
CAUTION: Do not operate the dishwasher when someone is taking a shower.	**OJO: No encienda el lavaplatos si alguien se está duchando.** (OH-hoh: NOH en-S'YEN-dah el lah-bah-PLAH-tohs see AHL-g'yen seh eh-stah doo-CHAHN-doh)

Cleaning the Oven

These are general instructions for operating a self-cleaning oven.

This is a self-cleaning oven.	**Este horno se limpia automáticamente.** (EH-steh OR-noh seh LEEMP-yah ah'oo-toh-mah-tee-kah-MEN-teh)
To clean the oven:	**Para limpiar el horno:** (pah-rah leemp-YAHR el OR-noh)
Remove these from the oven.	**Saque estos del horno.** (SAH-keh EH-stohs del OR-noh)
Lock the oven like this.	**Cierre el horno así.** (S'YEHR-reh el OR-noh ah-SEE)
Push the "On" button.	**Apriete el botón « ON ».** (ah-PR'YEH-teh el boh-TOHN « ON »)

Do not try to open the oven until the cycle is finished.

No intente abrir el horno hasta que el ciclo haya terminado.
(NOH een-TEN-teh ah-BREER el OR-noh ah-stah keh el SEE-kloh AH-yah tehr-mee-NAH-thoh)

Here are instructions for cleaning an oven manually:

To clean this oven . . .

Para limpiar este horno...
(pah-rah leemp-YAHR eh-steh OR-noh)

use this product.

use este producto.
(OO-seh EH-steh proh-THOOK-toh)

wear rubber gloves.

póngase guantes de goma.
(POHNG-gah-seh WAHN-tess deh GOH-mah)

Leave the cleaner for thirty minutes.

Deje el limpiador por treinta minutos.
(DEH-heh el leemp-yah-THOR por TRAIN-tah mee-NOO-tohs)

Wipe the cleaner off with a sponge.

Quite el limpiador con la esponja.
(KEE-teh el leemp-yah-THOR kohn lah eh-SPOHN-hah)

Be careful.

Tenga cuidado.
(TENG-gah kwee-THAH-thoh)

The cleaner burns the skin.

El limpiador quema la piel.
(el leemp-yah-THOR KEH-mah lah P'YELL)

67

Safety Precautions with Small Appliances

It's a good idea not to take it for granted that your employee knows how to handle all of your electrical appliances. Be sure to give basic safety instructions right from the beginning, even if they seem obvious to you.

Don't put electrical appliances in water.	**No ponga ningún aparato eléctrico en el agua.** (NOH POHNG-gah neeng-GOON ah-pah-RAH-toh eh-LEK-tree-koh en el AH- g'wah)
Disconnect small appliances before cleaning them.	**Desenchufe los aparatos pequeños antes de limpiarlos.** (dess-en-CHOO-feh lohs ah-pah-RAH-tohs peh-KEN-yohs AHN-tess deh leemp- YAHR-lohs)
Plug it in like this.	**Enchúfelo así.** (en-CHOO-feh-loh ah-SEE)
Unplug it like this.	**Desenchúfelo así.** (deh-sen-CHOO-feh-loh ah-SEE)
Don't pull the electrical cord.	**No tire el cordón.** (NOH-TEE-reh-el-kor-DOHN)
Don't use it.	**No lo use.** (NOH loh OO-seh)
It's broken.	**Está roto.** (eh-STAH ROH-toh)
It doesn't work.	**No funciona.** (NOH foon-S'YOH-nah)

It's dangerous.   **Es peligroso.**

                                    (ess-peh-lee-GROH-soh)

Danger Spots in the Kitchen

These phrases are important for maintaining safety in your home.

It's hot.   **Está caliente.**

                                    (eh-STAH kahl-YEN-teh)

It's slippery.   **Es resbaloso.**

                                    (ess ress-bah-LOH-soh)

It's not sturdy.   **No está firme.**

                                    (NOH eh-STAH FEER-meh)

It's heavy.   **Es pesado.**

                                    (ess peh-SAH-thoh)

It's fragile.   **Es frágil.**

                                    (ess FRAH-heel)

Don't touch it.   **No lo toque.**

                                    (NOH loh TOH-keh)

Be very careful with it.   **Tenga mucho cuidado.**

                                    (TENG-gah MOO-choh

                                    kwee-THAH-thoh)

The Bathroom

In restaurants you may see **Damas** (*Ladies*) and **Caballeros** (*Gentlemen*), but in the house, the name of this room is:

the bathroom   **el baño**

                                    (el BAHN-yoh)

Bathroom Chores

Here are some phrases for establishing the bathroom cleaning routine.

Put the dirty clothes in the laundry basket.	**Ponga la ropa sucia en la canasta.** (POHNG-gah lah ROH-pah SOO-s'yah en lah kah-NAH-stah)
the towels	**las toallas** (lahs TWAH-yahs)
the bathmat	**el tapete** (el tah-PEH-teh)
Put personal articles away.	**Ponga en su lugar los artículos de uso personal.** (POHNG-gah en soo loo-GAHR lohs ahr-TEE-koo-lohs deh OO-soh pehr-soh- NAHL)
Clean the mirrors.	**Limpie los espejos.** (LEEMP-yeh lohs eh-SPEH-hohs)
the walls	**las paredes** (lahs pah-REH-thess)
the toilet	**el inodoro** (el ee-noh-THOR-oh)
the sink	**el lavabo** (el lah-BAH-boh)
the counter top	**la superficie del tocador** (lah soo-pehr-FEE-s'yeh del toh-kah-THOR
the faucets	**las llaves del agua** (lahs YAH-bess-del-AH-gwah)

Specific Projects Around the House

the bathtub	**la bañera**
	(lah bahn-YEH-rah)
the rubber mat	**el tapete de hule**
	(el tah-PEH-teh deh OO-leh)
the shower	**la ducha**
	(lah DOO-chah)
the glass door	**la puerta de vidrio**
	(lah PWEHR-tah deh
	BEETHE-r'yoh)
the shower curtain	**la cortina de la ducha**
	(lah kor-TEE-nah deh lah
	DOO-chah)
the tile	**los azulejos**
	(lohs ah-soo-LEH-hohs)
the light fixtures	**las lámparas**
	(lahs LAHM-pah-rahs)
the floor	**el suelo**
	(el SWEH-loh)
the bathmats	**los tapetes**
	(lohs tah-PEH-tehs)
the scale	**la balanza**
	(lah bah-LAHN-sah)
the soap dish	**la jabonera**
	(lah hah-boh-NEH-rah)
the drinking glass	**el vaso**
	(el BAH-soh)
the wastebasket	**la canasta de la basura**
	(lah kah-NAH-stah deh lah
	bah-SOO-rah)

Cleaning Products and Equipment

Remember that you can substitute brand names for the underlined products.

Clean the mirrors with Windex.	**Limpie los espejos con Windex.**
	(LEEMP-yeh lohs eh-SPEH-hohs kohn WEEN-deh)
Use <u>this cleaner</u>.	**Use <u>este limpiador</u>.**
	(OO-seh EH-steh leemp-yah-THOR)
that product	**ese producto**
	(EH-seh proh-THOOK-toh)
the wet mop	**el trapeador mojado**
	(el trah-peh-ah-THOR moh-HAH-thoh)
the dry mop	**el trapeador seco**
	(el trah-peh-ah-THOR SEH-koh)
a wet rag	**un trapo mojado**
	(oon TRAH-poh moh-HAH-thoh)
a dry rag	**un trapo seco**
	(oon TRAH-poh SEH-koh)
the toilet brush	**el cepillo del inodoro**
	(el seh-PEE-yoh del ee-noh-THOR-oh)
the sponge	**la esponja**
	(lah eh-SPOHN-hah)

The Living Room

The Spanish word for *living room* is an easy one:

living room   **la sala**
                               (lah SAH-lah)

By adding one more word, you get *family room*:

family room   **la sala familiar**
                               (lah SAH-lah-fah-meel-YAHR)

The following phrases will help you give instructions for cleaning any living room or family room. Remember that you can put **No** before any of these instructions to tell someone *not* to do something.

Straightening and Rearranging

The following phrases are for explaining what you mean by "straightening" a room.

Straighten the room.   **Arregle esta habitación.**
                               (ahr-REH-gleh EH-stah
                               ah-bee-tah-S'YOHN)

Put items where they belong.   **Ponga las cosas en su lugar.**
                               (POHNG-gah lahs KOH-sahs en soo
                               loo-GAHR)

Move the furniture to clean <u>under</u> it. **Mueva los muebles para limpiar
                               debajo de ellos.**
                               (M'WEH-bah lohs M'WEH-bless pah-
                               rah leemp-YAHR deh-BAH-hoh deh
                               EH-yohs)

        in back of   **detrás de**
                                       (deh-TRAHS deh)

73

Things to Remove

The following phrases will help you explain what things you want to get rid of in your house.

Remove <u>the cobwebs</u>.	**Quite <u>las telarañas</u>.**
	(KEE-teh lahs teh-lah-RAHN-yahs)
these marks	**estas manchas**
	(EH-stahs MAHN-chahs)
this spot	**esta mancha**
	(EH-stah MAHN-chah)
the fingerprints	**estas huellas**
	(EH-stahs WEH-yahs)
the dust	**el polvo**
	(el POHL-boh)
the dirt	**la suciedad**
	(lah soo-s'yeh-THAHD)
the dog hair	**el pelo del perro**
	(el PEH-loh del PEHR-roh)
the cat hair	**el pelo del gato**
	(el PEH-loh del GAH-toh)
Empty the <u>ashtrays</u>.	**Vacíe los <u>ceniceros</u>.**
	(bah-SEE-eh lohs seh-nee-SEH-rohs)
trash cans	**las canastas de la basura**
	(lahs kah-NAH-stahs deh lah
	bah-SOO-rah)
Throw away the <u>dead flowers</u>.	**Tire a la basura las <u>flores muertas</u>.**
	(TEE-reh ah lah bah-SOO-rah lahs
	FLOR-ess-M'WEHR-tahs)
the trash	**la basura**
	(lah bah-SOO-rah)

Put the newspapers in this recycle bin.	**Ponga los periódicos en esta canasta para el reciclaje.**
	(POHNG-gah lohs peh-ree-OH-thee-kohs en EH-stah kah-NAH-stah pah-rah el reh-see-KLAH-heh)
the magazines	**las revistas**
	(lahs reh-BEE-stahs)
these papers	**estos papeles**
	(EH-stohs pah-PEH-less)
these boxes	**estas cajas**
	(EH-stahs KAH-hahs)
these bottles	**estas botellas**
	(EH-stahs boh-TEH-yahs)
these cans	**estas latas**
	(EH-stahs LAH-tahs)

Things to Clean

Here is a list of household items that often need the attention of a cleaner.

Clean the walls.	**Limpie las paredes.**
	(LEEMP-yeh lahs pah-REH-thehs)
the floor	**el suelo**
	(el SWEH-loh)
the windows	**las ventanas**
	(lahs ben-TAH-nahs)
the window screens	**la tela metálica de las ventanas**
	(lah TEH-lah meh-TAH-lee-kah deh lahs ben-TAH-nahs)

75

the baseboards	**los zócalos**
	(lohs SOH-kah-lohs)
the windowsills	**las repisas**
	(lahs reh-PEE-sahs)
the corners	**los rincones**
	(lohs reeng-KOH-ness)
the vents	**los escapes**
	(lohs eh-SKAH-pess)
the blinds	**las persianas**
	(lahs pehr-S'YAH-nahs)
the carpet	**la alfombra**
	(lah ahl-FOHM-brah)
the rugs	**las alfombras**
	(lahs ahl-FOHM-brahs)
the furniture made of <u>wood</u>	**los muebles de <u>madera</u>**
	(lohs M'WEH-blehs deh
	mah-THEH-rah)
metal	**metal**
	(meh-TAHL)
plastic	**plástico**
	(PLAHS-tee-koh)
glass	**vidrio**
	(BEE-thr'yoh)
the tables	**las mesas**
	(lahs MEH-sahs)
the piano	**el piano**
	(el P'YAH-noh)
the television	**el televisor**
	(el teh-leh-bee-SOR)

the electronic equipment	**el equipo electrónico** (el eh-KEE-poh eh-lek-TROH-nee-koh)
the upholstered furniture	**los muebles tapizados** (lohs M'WEH-bless tah-pee-SAH-thohs)
the armchairs	**los sillones** (lohs see-YOH-ness)
the footstool	**el taburete** (el tah-boo-REH-teh)
the sofa	**el sofá** (el soh-FAH)
the shelves	**los estantes** (lohs eh-STAHN-tess)
the pictures	**los cuadros** (lohs K'WAH-throhs)
the paintings	**las pinturas** (lahs peen-TOO-rahs)
the other ornaments	**los otros ornamentos** (lohs OH-trohs or-nah-MEN-tohs)
the light fixtures	**las lámparas** (lahs LAHM-pah-rahs)
the lamps	**las lámparas** (lahs LAHM-pah-rahs)
the lampshades	**las pantallas** (lahs pahn-TAH-yyahs)
the clock	**el reloj** (el reh-LOH)

the curtains	**las cortinas** (lahs kor-TEE-nahs)
the curtain rods	**las barras para las cortinas** (lahs BAHR-rahs pah-rah lahs kor-TEE-nahs)
the decorative objects	**los objetos decorativos** (lohs ohb-HEH-tohs deh-koh-rah-TEE-bohs)
the vase	**el florero** (el flor-EH-roh)
the planter	**la maceta** (lah ma-SEH-tah)
the mirror	**el espejo** (el eh-SPEH-hoh)
the fireplace equipment	**las herramientas para la chimenea** (lahs her-rah-M'YEN-tahs pah- rah lah chee-men-EH-ah)
the books	**los libros** (lohs LEE-brohs)

Cleaning Methods

You can combine the following cleaning tasks with the words in the previous section, simply by replacing the underlined word with the word you want.

Wash the curtains.	**Lave las cortinas.** (LAH-beh lahs kor-TEE-nahs)
Iron . . .	**Planche...** (PLAHN-cheh)

Hang . . .	**Cuelgue...**
	(K'WELL-geh)
Dust the furniture.	**Pásele el trapo a los muebles.**
	(PAH-seh-leh el TRAH-poh ah lohs
	M'WEH-bless)
Wipe . . .	**Pásele el trapo a...**
	(PAH-seh-leh el TRAH-poh ah)
Polish . . .	**Lustre...**
	(LOO-streh)
Vacuum the carpets.	**Pase la aspiradora por las alfombras.**
	(PAH-seh lah-ah- spee-rah-THOR-ah
	por lahs ahl-FOHM-brahs)
Sweep . . .	**Barra...**
	(BAHR-rah)
Spot-clean.	**Limpie las manchas.**
	(LEEM-p'yeh lahs MAHN-chahs)

Cleaning Equipment

Here are phrases for explaining what you would like your employee to use when cleaning different areas.

Use this to clean the walls.	**Use esto para limpiar las paredes.**
	(OO-seh EH-stoh pah-rah leemp-
	YAHR lahs pah-REH-thehs)
a rag	**un trapo**
	(oon TRAH-poh)
a damp cloth	**un trapo húmedo**
	(oon TRAH-poh OO-meh-thoh)

a brush	**un cepillo**
	(oon seh-PEE-yyoh)
a sponge	**una esponja**
	(OO-nah eh-SPOHN-hah)
a duster	**un plumero**
	(oon ploo-MEH-roh)
a dry mop	**un trapeador seco**
	(oon trah-peh-ah-THOR SEH-koh)
a wet mop	**un trapeador mojado**
	(oon trah-peh-ah-THOR moh-HAH-thoh)
the vacuum cleaner	**la aspiradora**
	(lah ah-spee-rah-THOR-ah)
the broom	**la escoba**
	(lah eh-SKOH-bah)
the floor polisher	**la enceradora de suelos**
	(lah en-seh-rah–THOR-ah deh SWEH-lohs)

Cleaning Products

These phrases are for specifying the type of cleaning products you would like your employee to use. You could also substitute the brand names of cleaning products here.

Use <u>water</u>	**Use <u>agua</u>**
	(OO-seh-AH-g'wah)
vinegar	**vinagre**
	(bee-NAH-greh)

ammonia	**amoníaco**
	(ah-moh-N'YAH-koh)
Windex	**Windex**
	(WEEN-deh)
furniture polish	**cera para muebles**
	(SEH-rah pah-rah M'WEH-bless)
wax	**cera**
	(SEH-rah)
the floor cleaner	**el limpiador de suelos**
	(el leemp-yah-THOR deh SWEH-lohs)
the spray cleaner	**el limpiador espray**
	(el leemp-yah-THOR eh-SPRY)
the carpet cleaner	**el limpiador de alfombras**
	(el leemp-yah-THOR deh ahl-FOHM-brahs)

The Dining Room

Following is the word for *dining room*—"a place to eat" in Spanish.

the dining room	**el comedor**
	(el koh-meh-THOR)

Dining Room Furniture

In this section you will find the names of typical dining room pieces. You may also want to refer to the section on living room furniture or to the glossary for more vocabulary choices.

the table	**la mesa**
	(lah MEH-sah)
the chairs	**las sillas**
	(lahs SEE-yyahs)
the buffet	**el aparador**
	(el ah-pah-rah-THOR)
the china cabinet	**la vitrina**
	(lah bee-TREE-nah)
the serving cart	**la mesa rodante**
	(lah MEH-sah roh-DAHN-teh)

Dining Room Chores

Following are typical chores specific to the dining room.

Set the table.	**Ponga la mesa.**
	(POHNG-gah lah MEH-sah)
Clear the table.	**Retire los platos.**
	(reh-TEE-reh lohs PLAH-tohs)
Throw away the dead flowers.	**Eche las flores muertas a la basura.**
	(EH-cheh lahs FLOR-ess-M'WEHR-tahs
	ah lah bah-SOO-rah
Arrange these flowers.	**Arregle estas flores.**
	(ah-REH-gleh EH-stahs FLOR-ess)
Remove spots <u>from the table</u>.	**Quite las manchas <u>de la mesa.</u>**
	(KEE-teh lahs MAHN-chahs deh lah
	MEH-sah)
from the tablecloth.	**del mantel.**
	(del mahn-TELL)
from the chair seats.	**de las sillas.**
	(deh lahs SEE-yyahs)

Specific Projects Around the House

Polish the furniture.	**Limpie los muebles con cera.** (LEEMP-yeh lohs M'WEH-bless kohn SEH-rah)
Clean the chandelier.	**Limpie la araña de luces.** (LEEMP-yeh lah–ah-RAHN-yah deh LOO-sess)
Polish the silver.	**Limple la plata.** (LEEMP-yeh lah PLAH-tah)
Wash the crystal.	**Lave el cristal.** (LAH-beh el krees-TAHL)
Put the silverware away.	**Ponga los cubiertos en su lugar.** (POHNG-gah lohs koo-B'YEHR-tohs en soo loo-GAHR)
Vacuum under the table.	**Pase la aspiradora por debajo de la mesa.** (PAH-seh lah-ah-spee-rah-THOR-ah por deh-BAH-hoh deh lah MEH-sah)
Dust the ceiling fan.	**Pase el trapo por el ventilador.** (PAH-seh-el TRAH-poh por el ben-tee-lah-THOR)

The Bedrooms

The Spanish word for *bedroom* is similar to the English word *dormitory*, but it's just one room, not the whole building!

the bedroom	**el dormitorio** (el dor-mee-TOR-yoh)

To make it plural, change **el** to **los,** and add **s.**

the bedrooms	**los dormitorios** (lohs dor-mee-TOR-yohs)

83

Bedroom Furniture

Following are the names of different types of bedroom furniture.

the bedroom furniture	**los muebles del dormitorio** (lohs M'WEH-bless del dor-mee-TOR-yoh)
the bed	**la cama** (lah KAH-mah)
the night table	**la mesa de noche** (lah MEH-sah deh NOH-cheh)
the lamps	**las lámparas** (lahs LAHM-pah-rahs)
the dresser	**el tocador** (el toh-kah-THOR)
the chest of drawers	**la cómoda** (lah KOH-moh-thah)
the wardrobe	**el armario** (el ahr-MAHR-yoh)
the jewelry box	**el joyero** (el hoh-YEH-roh)
the TV cabinet	**el mueble del televisor** (el M'WEH-bleh del teh-leh-bee-SOR)
the easy chair	**el sillón** (el see-YOHN)

Bedroom Chores

The following are typical bedroom cleaning chores. Remember that there are more cleaning terms in the living room section if you do not find what you need here.

Specific Projects Around the House

Dust the furniture. | **Pase el trapo por los muebles.**
(PAH-seh el TRAH-poh por lohs
M'WEH-bless)

the ceiling fan | **el ventilador**
(el ben-tee-lah-THOR)

the blinds | **las persianas**
(lahs pehr-S'YAH-nahs)

the framed photographs | **las fotografías enmarcadas**
(lahs foh-toh-grah-FEE-ahs
en-mahr-KAH-thahs)

the art objects | **los objetos decorativos**
(lohs ob-HEH-tohs
deh-koh-rah-TEE-bohs)

Make the bed. | **Arregle la cama.**
(ahr-REH-gleh lah KAH-mah)

Change the sheets. | **Cambie las sábanas.**
(KAHM-b'yeh lahs SAH-bah-nahs)

Wash the sheets. | **Lave las sábanas.**
(LAH-beh lahs SAH-bah-nahs)

the pillowcases | **las fundas**
(lahs FOON-dahs)

the blankets | **las cobijas**
(lahs koh-BEE-hahs)
las mantas
(lahs MAHN-tahs)
las frazadas
(lahs frah-SAH-thahs)

the bedspread | **la sobrecama**
(lah soh-breh-KAH-mah)

Closets and Clothing

A singular word is used in Spanish for *clothes*; the meaning is closer to *clothing* in English.

clothes / clothing   **la ropa**
                                   (lah ROH-pah)

And the word for *closet* is similar to *wardrobe* in English—a place to keep (or "guard") clothing:

the closet   **la guardarropa**
                                   (lah gwahr-thahr-ROH-pah)

In English, a *storage closet* is also an *armoire*, which is similar to the Spanish word:

the storage closet   **el armario**
                                   (el ahr-MAHR-yoh)

And in Spanish a *linen closet* is literally an "armoire for white clothing"!

the linen closet   **el armario para ropa blanca**
                                   (el ahr-MAHR-yoh pah-rah ROH-pah
                                   BLAHNG-kah)

Types of Clothing

The following phrases will help you identify different types of clothes.

the suits	**los trajes** (lohs TRAH-hess)
the jackets	**las chaquetas** (lahs chah-KEH-tahs)
the dresses	**los vestidos** (lohs bess-TEE-thohs)
the pants	**los pantalones** (lohs pahn-tah-LOH-ness)
the skirts	**las faldas** (lahs FAHL-thahs)
the shirts	**las camisas** (lahs kah-MEE-sahs)
the blouses	**las blusas** (lahs BLOO-sahs)
the belts	**los cinturones** (lohs seen-too-ROH-ness)
the neckties	**las corbatas** (lahs kor-BAH-tahs)
the sweaters	**los suéteres** (lohs SWEH-teh-ress)
the shoes	**los zapatos** (lohs sah-PAH-tohs)
the socks	**los calcetines** (lohs kahl-seh-TEE-ness)
the stockings	**las medias** (lahs MEH-th'yahs)

the underwear	**la ropa interior**
	(lah ROH-pah een-tehr-YOR)
the handbags	**las carteras**
	(lahs kahr-TEH-rahs)

Colors

You might want to identify your clothing (or other things in the house) by color. Say the name of the article first, then the color. For example, *red sweater* is **suéter rojo**. Also, the name of the color usually changes its ending to match the ending of the word it describes. For example, *red blouse* is **blusa roja** and *red blouses* would be **blusas rojas**.

red	**rojo**
	(ROH-hoh)
yellow	**amarillo**
	(ah-mah-REE-yoh)
blue	**azul**
	(ah-SOOL)
orange	**anaranjado**
	(ah-nah-rahn-HAH-thoh)
green	**verde**
	(BEHR-deh)
purple	**morado**
	(moh-RAH-thoh)
pink	**rosado**
	(roh-SAH-thoh)
brown	**marrón**
	(mahr-ROHN)
white	**blanco**
	(BLAHNG-koh)

black	**negro**
	(NEH-groh)
gray	**gris**
	(GREESE)

Putting Things Away

In this section you will find phrases that will help you tell your employee where to put things in your closets and drawers.

Hang up the clothes.	**Cuelgue la ropa.**
	(K'WELL-geh lah ROH-pah)
Hang the shirts here.	**Cuelgue las camisas aquí.**
	(K'WELL-geh lahs kah-MEE-sahs
	ah-KEE)
Put the shoes in the closet.	**Ponga los zapatos en la**
	guardarropa.
	(POHNG-gah lohs sah-PAH-tohs en
	lah gwahr-dahr-ROH-pah)
Put the sheets in the linen closet.	**Ponga las sábanas en el armario**
	para ropa blanca.
	(POHNG-gah lahs SAH-bah-nahs en
	el ahr-MAHR-yoh pah-rah ROH-pah
	BLAHNG-kah)
the pillow cases	**las fundas**
	(lahs FOON-dahs)
the towels	**las toallas**
	(lahs TWAH-yyahs)
these things	**estas cosas**
	(EH-stahs KOH-sahs)

on the shelf	**en la repisa**
	(en lah reh-PEE-sah)
in the drawer	**en el cajón**
	(en el kah-HOHN)
in the box	**en la caja**
	(en lah KAH-hah)
in the bag	**en la bolsa**
	(en lah BOHL-sah)
in the storage closet	**en el armario**
	(en el ahr-MAHR-yoh)
Put the dirty clothes in the hamper.	**Ponga la ropa sucia en la canasta.**
	(POHNG-gah lah ROH-pah SOO-s'yah
	en lah kah-NAH-stah)

The Laundry Room

The word for *laundry room* in Spanish is literally "a place for washing." It's also the name of the place where laundry can be done commercially.

the laundry room	**la lavandería**
	(lah lah-bahn-deh-REE-yah)

If your employee will be doing the laundry, you will want to give specific instructions for using your equipment as well as for washing different types of clothing.

The Washing Machine

If you still have the instructions for using your washing machine, you will most likely find that they are also written in Spanish. You might tape these to the wall near the machine for your employee to refer to. Below are some general instructions.

Turn on the <u>hot water</u>.	**Abra la llave del <u>agua caliente</u>.**
	(AH-brah lah YAH-beh del AH-g'wah kahl-YEN-teh)
cold water	**del agua fría**
	(del AH-g'wah FREE-ah)
Put the clothes in the washer.	**Ponga la ropa en la lavadora.**
	(POHNG-gah lah ROH-pah en lah lah-bah-THOR-ah)
Measure and add detergent.	**Mida y agregue detergente.**
	(MEE-thah ee ah-GREH-geh deh-tehr-HEN-teh)
Set the cycle.	**Seleccione el programa de lavado.**
	(seh-lek-S'YOH-neh el proh-GRAH-mah deh lah-BAH-thoh)
Set the size of load.	**Seleccione el tamaño de la tanda.**
	(seh-lek-S'YOH-neh el tah-MAHN-yoh deh lah TAHN-dah)
Set the timer.	**Ponga el reloj.**
	(POHNG-gah el reh-LOH)
Close the lid.	**Cierre la tapa.**
	(S'YEHR-reh lah TAH-pah)
Push the dial in.	**Empuje el indicador para dentro.**
	(em-POO-heh el een-dee-kah-THOR pah-rah DEN-troh)
Turn the dial to the right.	**Gire el indicador a la derecha.**
	(HEE-reh el een-dee-kah-THOR ah lah deh-REH-chah)

Go to "Start."

Pare donde indica « Start ».
(PAH-reh DOHN-deh een-DEE-kah
« Start »)

Then pull the dial out.

Y luego jale el indicador.
(ee L'WEH-goh HAH-leh el
een-dee-kah-THOR)

The machine will start.

La máquina se pondrá en marcha.
(lah MAH-kee-nah seh pohn-DRAH
en MAHR-chah)

Do not put your hands in the
machine while it is running.

**No ponga las manos adentro de la
máquina cuando está en marcha.**
(NOH POHNG-gah lahs MAH-nohs
ah-THEN-troh deh lah MAH-kee-nah
K'WAHN-doh eh-STAH en MAHR-chah)

When the cycle is completed,
remove the clothes from the
machine.

**Cuando el ciclo haya terminado,
saque la ropa de la máquina.**
(K'WAHN-doh el SEE-kloh AH-yah
tehr-mee-NAH-thoh SAH-keh lah
ROH-pah deh lah MAH-kee-nah)

Turn off the water faucets when
all the laundry is done.

**Cierre las llaves del agua cuando
haya terminado la lavandería.**
(S'YEHR-reh lahs YAH-behs del AH-
gwah kwahn-doh ah-yah tehr-mee-
NAH-thoh lah lah-bahn-deh-REE-ah)

CAUTION: Do not operate the
washing machine when
someone is taking a shower.

**OJO: No ponga en marcha la
lavadora si alguien se está
duchando.**
(OH-hoh NOH POHNG-gah en MAHR-
chah lah lah-bah-THOR-ah see AHL-
g'yen seh eh-STAH doo-CHAHN-doh)

Special Care Instructions

Be sure to tell your employee exactly what you want to be washed in the machine, and at what temperature. Show her how to separate the dark clothes from the light, and what kind of detergent to use. Be sure to specify whether or not to use bleach and/or fabric softener.

Separate the dark clothing from the light clothing.	**Separe la ropa oscura de la blanca.** (seh-PAH-reh lah ROH-pah ohs-KOO-rah deh lah BLAHNG-kah)
Spray stains with this product.	**Use este producto para quitar manchas.** (OO-seh EH-steh proh-THOOK-toh pah-rah kee-TAHR MAHN-chahs)
Fill the machine with dirty clothes to this level.	**Llene la máquina hasta aquí con ropa sucia.** (YEH-neh lah MAH-kee-nah AH-stah ah-KEE kohn ROH-pah SOO-s'yah)
Use <u>hot water</u> for white loads.	**Use agua caliente para las tandas de ropa blanca.** (OO-seh AH-g'wah kahl-YEN-teh pah-rah lahs TAHN-dahs deh ROH-pah BLAHNG-kah)
bleach	**lejía** (leh-HEE-ah)
fabric softener	**suavizante de telas** (swah-bee-SAHN-teh deh TEH-lahs)
Use cold water for dark loads.	**Use agua fría para la ropa oscura.** (OO-seh AH-g'wah FREE-ah pah-rah lah ROH-pah ohs-KOO-rah)

Do not use bleach.	**No use lejía.**
	(NOH OO-seh leh-HEE-ah)
Wash <u>the towels</u> separately from the clothing.	**Lave <u>las toallas</u> por separado.**
	(LAH-beh lahs TWAH-yahs por seh-pah-RAH-thoh)
the sheets	**las sábanas**
	(lahs SAH-bah-nahs)
Wash this on the gentle cycle.	**Use el ciclo suave para lavar esto.**
	(OO-seh el SEE-kloh SWAH-beh pah-rah lah-BAHR EH-stoh)
Do not wash this in the machine.	**No lave esto en la máquina.**
	(NOH LAH-beh EH-stoh en lah MAH-kee-nah)
Wash it by hand.	**Lávelo a mano.**
	(LAH-beh loh ah MAH-noh)
Do not leave the house while a machine is running.	**No salga de la casa mientras esté en marcha alguna máquina.**
	(NOH SAHL-gah deh lah KAH-sah M'YEN-trahs eh-STEH en MAHR-chah ahl-GOO-nah MAH-kee-nah)

The Dryer

Be sure to make it clear if you don't want certain items to be dried by machine.

Clean the lint filter, like this.	**Limpie el filtro así.**
	(LEEMP-yeh el FEEL-troh ah-SEE)

Specific Projects Around the House

Put the wet clothing in the dryer.
Ponga la ropa mojada en la secadora.
(POHNG-gah lah ROH-pah moh-HAH-thah en lah seh-kah-THOR-ah)

Set the drying time, like this.
Ponga el reloj así.
(POHNG-gah el reh-LOH ah-SEE)

Select the temperature, like this.
Seleccione la temperatura así.
(seh-lek-S'YOH-neh lah tem-peh-rah-TOO-rah ah-SEE)

Push the "On" button to start the machine.
Empuje el botón « On » para encender la máquina.
(ehm-POO-heh el boh-TOHN « On » pah-rah en-sen-DEHR lah MAH-kee- nah)

Remove the clothing promptly.
Saque la ropa en seguida.
(SAH-keh lah ROH-pah en seh-GEE-thah)

Fold the towels.
Doble las toallas.
(DOH-bleh lahs TWAH-yyahs)

the other items that don't need ironing
los otros artículos que no se planchan
(lohs OH-trohs ahr-TEE-koo-lohs keh noh seh PLAHN-chahn)

Hang this.
Cuelgue esto.
(K'WELL-geh EH-stoh)

Do not put this in the dryer.
No ponga esto en la secadora.
(NOH POHNG-gah EH-stoh en lah seh-kah-THOR-ah)

Lay it flat to dry, like this.	**Colóquelo así para que se seque.**
	(koh-LOH-keh-loh ah-SEE pah-rah keh seh SEH-keh)
Hang it on the clothesline.	**Tiéndalo en la cuerda de tender.**
	(T'YEN-dah-loh en lah K'WEHR-dah deh ten-DEHR)
Put the clean clothing away.	**Ponga la ropa limpia en su lugar.**
	(POHNG-gah lah ROH-pah LEEMP-yah en soo loo-GAHR)
Wipe the top of the washer and dryer.	**Pase el trapo por la superficie de las máquinas.**
	(PAH-seh el TRAH-poh por lah soo-pehr-FEE-s'yeh deh lahs MAH-kee-nahs)

Ironing Instructions

It's always best to avoid disasters before they happen, by explaining how your iron works for different fabrics, whether or not you want to use starch, and giving any special instructions.

Iron only on the ironing board.	**Planche solamente en el burro de planchar.**
	(PLAHN-cheh soh-lah-MEN-teh en el BOOR-roh deh plahn-CHAR)
Fill the iron with water, like this.	**Llene la plancha con agua así.**
	(YEH-neh lah PLAHN-chah kohn AH-g'wah ah-SEE)

Specific Projects Around the House

Use a <u>hot iron</u> for this.	**Use la <u>plancha caliente</u> para esto.**
	(OO-seh lah PLAHN-chah kahl-YEN-teh pah-rah EH-stoh)
cool iron	**la plancha templada**
	(lah PLAHN-chah tehm-PLAH-thah)
Do not iron this.	**No planche esto.**
	(NOH PLAHN-cheh EH-stoh)
Do not iron clothing that has spots.	**No planche la ropa si tiene manchas.**
	(NOH PLAHN-cheh lah ROH-pah see t'yeh-neh MAHN-chahs)
Never let the iron rest in a flat position.	**No deje la plancha acostada.**
	(NOH DEH-heh lah PLAHN-chah ah-koh-STAH-thah)
Let the iron rest on its end.	**Deje la plancha parada.**
	(DEH-heh lah PLAHN-chah pah-RAH-thah)
Sprinkle this with water.	**Salpique esto con agua.**
	(sahl-PEE-keh EH-stoh kohn AH-g'wah)
Spray starch on this.	**Ponga almidón espray en esto.**
	(POHNG-gah ahl-mee-THOHN eh-SPRY en EH-stoh)
Unplug the iron when you finish.	**Desenchufe la plancha cuando termine.**
	(dess-en-CHOO-feh lah PLAHN-chah K'WAHN-doh tehr-MEE-neh)
Empty the iron of water.	**Vacíe la plancha.**
	(bah-SEE-eh lah PLAHN-chah)

97

Let the iron cool before putting it away.	**Deje que la plancha se enfríe antes de ponerla en su lugar.** (DEH-heh keh lah PLAHN-chah seh en-FREE-eh AHN-tess deh poh-NEHR-lah esn soo loo-GAHR)

The Home Office

The office at home could be called **la oficina**, but it is more common to use a different word:

the office	**el despacho** (el deh-SPAH-choh)

General cleaning tasks are the same as for other rooms. Following are the names of typical objects found in home offices.

Office Furniture and Equipment

the desk	**el escritorio** (el eh-skree-TOH-r'yoh)
the chair	**la silla** (lah SEE-yyah)
the table	**la mesa** (lah MEH-sah)
the bookshelves	**los estantes** (lohs eh-STAHN-tess)
the filing cabinet	**el archivador** (ehl ahr-chee-bah-THOR)
the lamp	**la lámpara** (lah LAM-pah-rah)

Specific Projects Around the House

the computer	**la computadora**
	(lah kohm-poo-tah-THOR-ah)
the computer screen	**la pantalla**
	(lah pahn-TAH-yyah)
the keyboard	**el teclado**
	(el teh-KLAH-thoh)
the laptop	**la computadora portátil**
	(lah kohm-poo-tah-THOR-ah-
	por-TAH-teel)
the printer	**la impresora**
	(lah eem-preh-SOR-ah)
the copier	**la fotocopiadora**
	(lah foh-toh-koh-p'yah-THOR-ah)
the fax machine	**el fax**
	(el FAHKS)
the shredder	**la trituradora**
	(lah tree-too-rah-THOR-ah)
the telephone	**el teléfono**
	(el teh-LEH-foh-noh)
the clock	**el reloj**
	(el reh-LOH)
the stapler	**la grapadora**
	(lah grah-pah-THOR-ah)
the scissors	**las tijeras**
	(lahs tee-HEH-rahs)
the scotch tape	**la cinta**
	(lah SEEN-tah)
office supplies	**los artículos de oficina**
	(lohs ahr-TEE-koo-lohs deh
	oh-fee-SEE-nah)

paper	**el papel**
	(el pah-PELL)
pencils	**los lápices**
	(lohs LAH-pee-sess)
pens	**las plumas**
	(lahs PLOO-mahs)
important documents	**los documentos importantes**
	(lohs doh-koo-MEN-tohs-eem-por-
	TAHN-tess)
books	**los libros**
	(lohs LEE-brohs)
wastepaper basket	**la cesta de la basura**
	(lah SESS-tah deh lah bah-SOO-rah)

Cleaning the Home Office

Following are phrases that will help you explain how you would like your office to be cleaned.

Straighten the top of the desk.	**Arregle las cosas que estén encima del escritorio.**
	(ahr-REH-gleh lahs KOH-sahs keh eh-STÉN en-SEE-mah del eh-skree-TOR-yoh)
Put the supplies in place.	**Ponga los artículos de oficina en su lugar.**
	(POHNG-gah lohs ahr-TEE-koo-lohs deh oh-fee-SEE-nah en soo loo-GAHR)

Specific Projects Around the House

Don't touch these papers.

No toque estos documentos.
(NOH TOH-keh EH-stohs
doh-koo-MEN-tohs)

Empty the wastebasket.

Vacíe la cesta de la basura.
(bah-SEE-eh lah SEH-stah deh lah
bah-SOO-rah)

Don't use chemical cleaners on
the electronic equipment.

**No use limpiadores químicos en el
equipo electrónico.**
(NOH OO-seh leemp-yah-THOR-ehs
KEE-mee-kohs en el eh-KEE-poh
eh-lek- TROH-nee-koh)

Chapter 5

Child Care

The English expression *child care* is translated into Spanish as "the care of children":

child care

el cuidado de los niños
(el kwee-THAH-thoh deh lohs NEEN-yohs)

A person who devotes her time to the care of children is:

the nanny / babysitter

la niñera
(lah neenYEH-rah)

Important Guidelines

Very explicit instructions and warnings are important for people taking care of children. It is better to spell out what you expect, even if it seems obvious to you. Customs here may not be obvious to a newcomer to this country.

Establishing Priorities

The following phrases will help you explain what is most important to you in the care of your children.

The children's health and safety come first.	**La salud y la seguridad de los niños es primordial.**
	(lah sah-LOOD ee lah seh-goo-ree-THAHD deh lohs NEEN-yohs es pree-mor-D'YAHL)
The care of the children is more important than cleaning the house.	**El cuidado de los niños es más importante que la limpieza de la casa.**
	(el kwee-THAH-thoh deh lohs NEEN-yohs es MAHS eem-por-TAHN-teh keh lah leemp-YEH-sah deh lah KAH-sah)
Always ask before trying any new activity.	**Siempre pregunte antes de hacer alguna actividad nueva.**
	(S'YEM-preh preh-GOON-teh AHN-tess deh ah-SEHR ahl-GOO-nah ahk-tee-bee-THAHD N'WEH-bah)
Tell me if you have <u>problems</u>.	**Si tiene <u>problemas</u>, hable conmigo.**
	(see T'YEH-neh proh-BLEH-mahs AH-bleh kohn-MEE-goh)
questions	**preguntas**
	(preh-GOON-tahs)

Emergencies

You will probably want to leave emergency information written down for your babysitter. This could be posted next to the telephone, or perhaps in the children's room.

Call <u>me</u> in case of an emergency.

Llámeme en el caso de una emergencia.
(YAH-meh-meh en el KAH-soh deh OO-nah eh-mehr-HEN-s'yah)

911

nueve-uno-uno
(N'WEH-beh OO-noh OO-noh)

this number

este número
(EH-steh NOO-meh-roh)

Safety

As every household is different, you will want to give specific instructions about what is safe and what may be dangerous in your child's surroundings. Following are phrases to help you communicate your wishes and your concerns.

Be in the room with the child at all times.

Esté en la misma habitación con el niño en todo momento.
(eh-STEH en lah MEES-mah ah-bee-tah-S'YOHN kohn el NEEN-yoh en TOH-thoh moh-MEN-toh)

Do not leave the children alone with another person, even for a minute.	**No deje a los niños solos con otra persona, ni por un momento.** (NOH DEH-heh ah lohs NEEN-yohs SOH-lohs kohn OH-trah pehr-SOH-nah NI por oon moh-MEN-toh)
Do not leave the children alone in a car.	**No deje solos a los niños en un carro.** (NOH DEH-heh SOH-lohs ah lohs NEEN-yohs en oon KAHR-roh)
Keep children away from <u>the fireplace</u>.	**Mantenga a los niños lejos de <u>la chimenea</u>.** (mahn-TENG-gah ah lohs NEEN-yohs LEH-hohs deh lah chee-meh-NEH-ah)
the heating unit	**la calefacción** (lah kah-leh-fahk-S'YOHN)
the stove	**la estufa** (lah eh-STOO-fah)
the appliances	**los aparatos eléctricos** (lohs ah-pah-RAH-tohs eh-LEK-tree-kohs)
the electrical outlets	**los enchufes** (lohs en-CHOO-fess)
small objects	**los objetos pequeños** (lohs ohb-HEH-tohs peh-KEN-yohs)
medicines	**las medicinas** (lahs meh-thee-SEE-nahs)
chemicals	**las químicas** (lahs KEE-mee-kahs)

Child Care

cleaning supplies	**los limpiadores**
	(lohs leemp-yah-THOR-ess)
unfamiliar animals	**animales desconocidos**
	(lohs ah-nee-MAH-less
	dehs-koh-noh-SEE-thohs)
the street	**la calle**
	(lah KAH-yeh)
Always ask before taking the children out of the house.	**Pregunte antes de llevar a los niños afuera.**
	(preh-GOON-teh AHN-tess deh yeh-BAHR ah lohs NEEN-yohs ah-FWEH-rah)
Hold the child's hand when crossing the street.	**Agarre la mano del niño mientras crucen la calle.**
	(ah-GAHR-reh lah MAH-noh del NEEN-yoh M'YEN-trahs KROO-sen lah KAH-yeh)
Do not let children play outside unsupervised.	**No deje que los niños jueguen afuera sin vigilar.**
	(NOH DEH-heh keh lohs NEEN-yohs H'WEH-ghen ah-F'WEH-rah SEEN bee-hee-LAHR)
Do not let children accept candy or gifts from strangers.	**No deje que los niños acepten dulces o regalos de gente desconocida.**
	(NOH DEH-heh keh lohs NEEN-yohs ah-SEP-ten DOOL-sess oh reh-GAH-lohs deh HEN-teh dess-koh-noh-SEE-thah)

Discipline

How you discipline your children is very personal. The following phrases are meant to help you give guidelines to your babysitter as to how you would like your children to be treated.

Always treat the children with affection.	**Siempre trate a los niños con cariño.**
	(S'YEM-preh TRAH-teh ah lohs NEEN-yohs kohn kah-REEN-yoh)
Be firm.	**Manténgase firme.**
	(mahn-TENG-gah-seh FEER-meh)
Advise me of children's misbehavior.	**Avíseme si los niños no se portan bien.**
	(ah-BEE-seh-meh see lohs NEEN-yohs noh seh POR-tahn B'YEN)
Do not <u>spank</u> the children.	**No <u>pegue</u> a los niños.**
	(NOH PEH-geh ah lohs NEEN-yohs)
punish	**castigue**
	(kahs-TEE-geh)
threaten	**amenace**
	(ah-meh-NAH-seh)
frighten	**espante**
	(eh-SPAHN-teh)
yell at	**les grite**
	(lehs GREE-teh)
talk about religion with	**hable de religión con**
	(AH-bleh deh reh-lee-H'YOHN kohn)

What you ask your babysitter to do will obviously depend on the ages of your children and on their special needs. The phrases in the following sections can be adapted by substituting other words so that you can customize your instructions. Remember that you can put **No** before any of these instructions.

Caring for Babies

If the baby is a girl, she is **la bebé**; if he's a boy, he is **el bebé**. (If **el** follows **a**, it should be contracted to **al**. *Her* is **la**, and *him* is **lo**, and sometimes both *her* and *him* are **le**. The phrases that follow practice all of these forms.

Feeding and Changing Diapers

The following phrases will help you communicate exactly how you expect your baby to be taken care of.

Feed the baby . . .	**Déle de comer al / (a la) bebé...**
	(DEH-leh deh koh-MEHR ahl / (ah lah) beh-BEH)
at ten o'clock A.M.	**a las diez de la mañana.**
	(ah lahs D'YESS deh lah mahn-YAH-nah)
when s/he cries.	**cuando llore.**
	(K'WAHN-doh YOH-reh)
Heat the bottle.	**Caliente el biberón un poco.**
	(kah-L'YEN-teh ehl bee-beh-ROHN oon POH-koh)

Burp the baby.	**Haga eructar al / (a la) bebé.**
	(AH-gah eh-rook-TAHR ahl / (ah lah) beh-BEH)
Wipe his/her face.	**Límpiele la cara.**
	(LEEMP-yeh-leh lah KAH-rah)
Change his/her diaper . . .	**Cámbiele el pañal...**
	(KAHM-b'yeh-leh el pahn-YAHL)
every two hours.	**cada dos horas.**
	(KAH-thah DOHS OH-rahs)
when there is a dirty diaper.	**cuando haya un pañal sucio.**
	(K'WAHN-doh AH-yah oon pahn-YAHL SOOSE-yoh)
wet	**mojado**
	(moh-HAH-thoh)
Put the dirty diapers here.	**Ponga los pañales sucios aquí.**
	(POHNG-gah lohs pahn-YAH-less SOOSE-yohs ah-KEE)
Use this product.	**Use este producto.**
	(OO-seh EH-steh proh-THOOK-toh)

Taking the Baby Out

If you want your babysitter to take the baby for walks, these phrases will help you set guidelines.

Take the baby out in the baby carriage.	**Lleve al / (a la) bebé afuera en el cochecito.**
	(YEH-beh al / (ah lah) beh-BEH ah-F'WEH-rah en el koh-cheh-SEE-toh)
the stroller	**la sillita**
	(lah see-YEE-tah)

Stay on the sidewalk.

Quédese en la acera.
(KEH-theh-seh en lah-ah-SEH-rah)

Be very careful crossing the street.

Tenga mucho cuidado al cruzar la calle.
(TENG-gah moo-choh kwee-THAH-thoh ahl kroo-SAHR lah KAH-yeh)

Bathing and Putting the Baby to Bed

Following are phrases that give guidelines for bathtime and bedtime.

Give the baby a bath . . .

Dale un baño al / (a la) bebé...
(DAH-leh oon BAHN-yoh ahl / (ah lah) beh-BEH)

in the morning.

en la mañana.
(en lah mahn-YAH-nah)

the afternoon.

la tarde.
(lah TAHR-deh)

before putting him / her to bed.

antes de acostarlo / acostarla.
(AHN-tess deh ah-kohs-TAHR-loh / lah)

Never leave the baby alone in the bath.

Nunca deje solo (sola) en el baño al (a la) bebé.
(NOONG-kah DEH-heh SOH-loh en ehl BAH-n'yoh ahl beh-BEH)

Use tepid water.

Use agua tibia.
(OO-seh AH-g'wah TEEB-yah)

Wash his / her hair with this shampoo.

Lávele el pelo con este champú.
(LAH-beh-leh el PEH-loh kohn EH-steh chahm-POO)

111

Wrap him / her in a towel.	**Envuélvalo / Envuélvala en una toalla.**
	(en-B'WELL-bah-loh en oo-nah TWAH-yah)
Don't let the baby get cold.	**No deje que se enfríe el / (la) bebé.**
	(NOH DEH-heh keh seh en-FREE-eh el beh-BEH)
Dress him / her in these pajamas.	**Póngale este piyama.**
	(POHNG-gah-leh EH-steh pee-YAH-mah)
this shirt	**esta camisa**
	(EH-stah kah-MEE-sah)
this outfit	**este conjunto**
	(EH-steh kohn-HOON-toh)
Put the baby in the crib at eight o'clock.	**Acuéstele al / (a la) bebé en la cuna a las ocho.**
	(ah-K'WESS-teh-leh ahl beh-BEH en lah KOO-nah ah lahs OH-choh)
If the baby cries, pick him / her up.	**Si el / (la) bebé llora, recógelo / recógela.**
	(see el beh-BEH YOH-rah reh-KOH-heh-loh)
Rock the baby.	**Acune al / (a la) bebé en la mecedora.**
	(ah KOON-neh ahl beh-BEH en lah meh-seh-THOR-ah)

Caring for Toddlers and Older Children

Again, if the child is a boy, he will be **el niño**; a girl is **la niña**. *Him* is **lo**, and *her* is **la**, while both *him* and *her* are sometimes **le**. Any combination of boys and girls are **los niños**, while two or more girls are **las niñas**.

Preparing Meals

This is another extremely personal matter. These phrases will help you explain how your children should be fed.

The children should eat everything on their plates.	**Los niños deben comer todo lo que esté en el plato.** (lohs NEEN-yohs DEH-ben koh-MEHR TOH-thoh loh keh eh-STEH en el PLAH-toh)
Don't worry if they don't eat everything.	**No se preocupe si no lo comen todo.** (NOH seh preh-oh-KOO-peh see noh loh KOH-men TOH-thoh)
If they don't eat this, . . .	**Si no comen esto,...** (see noh KOH-men EH-stoh)
offer them that.	**ofrézcales eso.** (oh-FRESS-kah-less EH-so)
don't give them anything else.	**no les dé otra cosa.** (NOH less DEH OH-trah KOH-sah)
dessert	**el postre** (el POHS-treh)

candy	**dulces**
	(DOOL-sess)
Prepare the children's <u>breakfast</u>.	**Prepare el desayuno para los niños.**
	(preh-PAH-reh el deh-sah-YOO-noh pah-rah lohs NEEN-yohs)
lunch	**el almuerzo**
	(el ahl-M'WEHR-soh)
dinner	**la cena**
	(lah SEH-nah)
a snack	**un antojito**
	(oon ahn-toh-HEE-toh)
a drink	**algo de beber**
	(AHL-goh deh beh-BEHR)
this medicine	**esta medicina**
	(EH-stah meh-dee-SEE-nah)
Don't give him / her this.	**No le dé esto.**
	(NOH leh DEH EH-stoh)
Clear the table.	**Retire los platos de la mesa.**
	(reh-TEE-reh lohs PLAH-tohs deh lah MEH-sah)
Wash the dishes.	**Lave los platos.**
	(LAH-beh lohs PLAH-tohs)
Throw this away.	**Bote esto a la basura.**
	(BOH-teh EH-stoh ah lah bah-SOO-rah)

Bathing and Getting Children Dressed

Following are phrases relating to bathing and dressing the children. Be sure to specify what kind of clothing you want your children to wear for specific occasions. These phrases will also help you show your babysitter what the children need to do at bath time and where to find their clothing.

You might want to review the names for different types of clothing on page 87, or in the glossary at the back of the book.

It's important that the children take a bath.

Es importante que los niños se bañen.

(ess eem-por-TAHN-teh keh lohs NEEN-yohs seh BAHN-yen)

Stay in the bathroom with the children while they are bathing.

Quédese en el baño con los niños mientras se bañen.

(KEH-theh-seh en el BAHN-yoh kohn lohs NEEN-yohs M'YEN-trahs seh BAHN-yen)

Watch the children while they are in the tub.

Vigile a los niños mientras estén en la tina.

(bee-HEE-leh ah lohs NEEN-yohs M'YEN-trahs eh-STEN en lah TEE-nah)

Make sure they brush their teeth.

Haga que los niños se laven los dientes.

(AH-gah keh lohs NEEN-yohs seh LAH-ben lohs D'YEN-tess)

Comb his / her hair.

Péinele el pelo.

(PAY-neh-leh el PEH-loh)

Braid her hair.

Hágale trenzas.

(AH-gah-leh TREN-sahs)

Put her hair in a ponytail.

Póngale el pelo en cola de caballo.

(POHNG-gah-leh el PEH-loh en KOH-lah deh kah-BAH-yoh)

Help them get dressed.
Ayúdelos a vestirse.
(ah-YOO-theh-lohs ah beh-STEER-seh)

get undressed.
a desvestirse.
(ah dess-beh-STEER-seh)

Button the shirt.
Abotone la camisa.
(ah-boh-TOH-neh lah kah-MEE-sah)

Tie the sash.
Átele la faja.
(AH-teh-leh lah FAH-hah)

shoes
los zapatos
(lohs sah-PAH-tohs)

Put her socks on.
Póngale los calcetines.
(POHNG-gah-leh lohs
kahl-seh-TEE-ness)

The children's clothing is here.
La ropa de los niños está aquí.
(lah ROH-pah deh lohs NEEN-yohs eh-
STAH ah-KEE)

in this drawer.
en este cajón.
(en EH-steh kah-HOHN)

the closet.
la guardarropa.
(lah gwahr-dahr-ROH-pah)

the cabinet.
el gabinete.
(el gah-bee-NEH-teh)

Put the dirty clothes here.
Ponga la ropa sucia aquí.
(POHNG-gah lah ROH-pah SOOSE-
yah ah-KEE)

in the hamper.
en la canasta para ropa sucia.
(en lah kah-NAH-stah pah-rah
ROH-pah SOOSE-yah)

Playtime

You may want to take advantage of this opportunity for your children to learn Spanish while they are young. If so, encourage your babysitter to speak to them in Spanish. Here are some phrases for giving instructions for playtime.

Speak to the children in Spanish.	**Hable con los niños en español.** (AH-bleh kohn lohs NEEN-yohs en eh-spahn-YOHL)
Read to the children in Spanish.	**Lea a los niños en español.** (LEH-ah ah lohs NEEN-yohs en eh-spahn-YOHL)
Play with the children.	**Juegue con los niños.** (H'WEH-geh kohn lohs NEEN-yohs)
The toys are here.	**Los juguetes están aquí.** (lohs hoo-GEH-tess eh-STAHN ah-KEE)
If the children fight over a toy . . .	**Si los niños se pelean por un juguete...** (see lohs NEEN-yohs seh peh-LEH-ahn por oon hoo-GEH-teh)
separate them.	**sepáreles.** (seh-PAH-reh-less)
take the toy away from both of them.	**Quíteles el juguete a los dos.** (KEE-teh-less el hoo-GEH-teh ah lohs DOHS)
try to interest them in another activity.	**Trate de interesarles en otra actividad.** (TRAH-teh deh een-teh-reh-SAHR-less en OH-trah ahk-tee-bee-THAHD)

117

Put the toys away.	**Ponga los juguetes en su lugar.**
	(POHNG-gah lohs hoo-GEH-tess en soo loo-GAHR)
Straighten the children's room.	**Arregle el cuarto de los niños.**
	(ar-REH-gleh el K'WAHR-toh deh lohs NEEN-yohs)
The children may (not) play here.	**Los niños (no) deben jugar aquí.**
	(lohs NEEN-yohs [NOH] DEH-ben-hoo-gahr ah-KEE)
The children may watch <u>TV</u>.	**Los niños pueden ver la televisión.**
	(lohs NEEN-yohs PWEH-then behr lah teh-leh-bee-S'YOHN)
<u>this program</u> only.	**este programa solamente.**
	(EH-steh proh-GRAH-mah soh-lah-MEN-teh)
for <u>thirty minutes</u>.	**por treinta minutos.**
	(por TRAIN-tah mee-NOO-tohs)
before they go to bed.	**antes de acostarse.**
	(AHN-tess deh ah-koh-STAHR-seh)
The children must not watch TV.	**Los niños no deben ver la televisión.**
	(lohs NEEN-yohs NOH DEH-ben behr lah teh-leh-bee-S'YOHN)

Putting Children to Bed

Put the children to bed at eight o'clock.	**Acueste a los niños a las ocho.**
	(ah-K'WESS-teh ah lohs NEEN-yohs ah lahs OH-choh)

Child Care

If the children cry . . .

Si lloran los niños...
(see YOH-rahn lohs NEEN-yohs)

    try to calm them down.

    trate de calmarlos.
    (TRAH-teh deh
    kahl-MAHR-lohs)

    give him / her a glass of water.

    déle un vaso de agua.
    (DEH-leh oon BAH-soh deh
    AH-g'wah)

Appendix

Numbers

0	cero		18	dieciocho
1	uno		19	diecInueve
2	dos			
3	tres			
4	cuatro		20	veinte
5	cinco		21	veintiuno
6	seis		22	veintidós
7	siete		23	veintitrés
8	ocho		24	veinticuatro
9	nueve		25	veinticinco
10	diez		26	veintiséis
			27	veintisiete
			28	veintiocho
11	once		29	veintinueve
12	doce			
13	trece			
14	catorce		30	treinta
15	quince		31	treinta y uno
16	dieciséis		32	treinta y dos
17	diecisiete		33	treinta y tres

Appendix

34	treinta y cuatro		60	sesenta
35	treinta y cinco		61	sesenta y uno
36	treinta y seis		62	sesenta y dos
37	treinta y siete		63	sesenta y tres
38	treinta y ocho		64	sesenta y cuatro
39	treinta y nueve		65	sesenta y cinco
			66	sesenta y seis
			67	sesenta y siete
40	cuarenta		68	sesenta y ocho
41	cuarenta y uno		69	sesenta y nueve
42	cuarenta y dos			
43	cuarenta y tres			
44	cuarenta y cuatro		70	setenta
45	cuarenta y cinco		71	setenta y uno
46	cuarenta y seis		72	setenta y dos
47	cuarenta y siete		73	setenta y tres
48	cuarenta y ocho		74	setenta y cuatro
49	cuarenta y nueve		75	setenta y cinco
			76	setenta y seis
			77	setenta y siete
50	cincuenta		78	setenta y ocho
51	cincuenta y uno		79	setenta y nueve
52	cincuenta y dos			
53	cincuenta y tres			
54	cincuenta y cuatro		80	ochenta
55	cincuenta y cinco		81	ochenta y uno
56	cincuenta y seis		82	ochenta y dos
57	cincuenta y siete		83	ochenta y tres
58	cincuenta y ocho		84	ochenta y cuatro
59	cincuenta y nueve		85	ochenta y cinco

Numbers

86	**ochenta y seis**	167	**ciento sesenta y siete**
87	**ochenta y siete**	179	**ciento setenta y**
88	**ochenta y ocho**		**nueve**
89	**ochenta y nueve**	188	**ciento ochenta y ocho**
		194	**ciento noventa y**
			cuatro
90	**noventa**		
91	**noventa y uno**		
92	**noventa y dos**	200	**doscientos**
93	**noventa y tres**	300	**trescientos**
94	**noventa y cuatro**	400	**cuatrocientos**
95	**noventa y cinco**	500	**quinientos**
96	**noventa y seis**	600	**seiscientos**
97	**noventa y siete**	700	**setecientos**
98	**noventa y ocho**	800	**ochocientos**
99	**noventa y nueve**	900	**novecientos**

100	**cien**	1000	**mil**
101	**ciento uno**	2000	**dos mil**
102	**ciento dos**	2009	**dos mil nueve**
114	**ciento catorce**	40,000	**cuarenta mil**
129	**ciento veintinueve**	1999	**mil novecientos**
133	**ciento treinta y tres**		**noventa y nueve**
142	**ciento cuarenta y dos**		
156	**ciento cincuenta y**		
	seis	1,000,000	**un millón**

English-Spanish Glossary

The glossaries below include all the words in the book, arranged in alphabetical order, first in English, and then in Spanish. You may find it handy to look up an individual word here, find the page number(s) where it is used in the text, and then refer to the text for a complete phrase.

Expressions

A.M.	de la mañana
Be careful.	Cuidado. / Tenga cuidado.
Call 911.	Llame al nueve-uno-uno.
Don't . . .	No...
Excuse me.	Disculpe.
For how long . . .	¿Por cuánto tiempo... ?
God willing.	¡Ojalá!
Good afternoon.	Buenas tardes.
Good evening.	Buenas tardes / noches.
Good morning.	Buenos días.
Good night.	Buenas noches.
Good-bye.	Adiós.
Hello.	Hola.
How . . . ?	¿Cómo... ?
How are you?	¿Cómo está usted?
How do you say . . . ?	¿Cómo se dice... ?
How many . . . ?	¿Cuántos... ?
How much . . . ?	¿Cuánto... ?
I'm sorry.	Lo siento.
No.	No.
P.M.	de la tarde / de la noche
Please.	Por favor.

See you later.	Hasta luego.
Thank you.	Gracias.
Until when … ?	¿Hasta cuándo… ?
Welcome.	Bienvenido.
What … ?	¿Cuál… ?
What … ?	¿Qué… ?
What for … ?	¿Para qué… ?
When … ?	¿Cuándo… ?
Where … ?	¿Dónde… ?
Where (to) … ?	¿Adónde… ?
Who … ?	¿Quién… ?
Whose … ?	¿De quién… ?
Why … ?	¿Por qué?
With whom … ?	¿Con quién… ?
Yes.	Sí.
You're welcome.	De nada.

People

baby	bebé
babysitter	niñera
boss	jefe, jefa / patrón, patrona
boyfriend	novio
brother	hermano
child	niño, niña
children	niños, niñas
children (sons and daughters)	hijos, hijas
daughter	hija
father	papá / padre
friend	amigo, amiga
girlfriend	novia
he	él
her	la / le / a ella
him	lo / le / a él
husband	esposo
I	yo
mother	mamá / madre
neighbor	vecino, vecina
parents	padres
she	ella
sister	hermana
someone	alguien
son	hijo

stranger	persona desconocida
they	ellos / ellas
we	nosotros / nosotras
wife	esposa
you	usted
you (all)	ustedes

Places

basement	sótano
bathroom	baño
bedroom	dormitorio / cuarto / recámara
bus stop	parada de autobuses
cabinet	gabinete
closet (clothes)	guardarropa
closet (linen)	armario para la ropa blanca
closet (storage)	armario
dining room	comedor
family room	sala familiar
garage	garaje
hall	pasillo
kitchen	cocina
laundry room	lavandería
library	biblioteca
living room	sala
nursery	cuarto de los niños
office	despacho / oficina
pantry	despensa
park	parque
patio	patio
place	lugar
playroom	cuarto de recreo
porch	porche
room	habitación
utility room	lavandería

Words That Describe People, Places, or Things

Note: the endings of these words may change to match the gender or number of the words they describe.

English-Spanish Glossary

bad	malo (-a), (-os), (-as)
big	grande, grandes
broken	roto (-a), (-os), (-as)
calm	tranquilo (-a), (-os), (-as)
clean	limpio (-a), (-os), (-as)
cloudy	nublado
cold	frío (-a), (-os), (-as)
cool	templado
damp	húmedo (-a), (-os), (-as)
dangerous	peligroso (-a), (-os), (-as)
dark	oscuro (-a), (-os), (-as)
dead	muerto (-a), (-os), (-as)
dirty	sucio (-a), (-os), (-as)
dry	seco (-a), (-os), (-as)
empty	vacío (-a), (-os), (-as)
fired (from a job)	despedido (-a), (-os), (-as)
flat (position)	acostado (-a), (-os), (-as)
fragile	frágil, frágiles
good	bueno (-a), (-os), (-as)
happy	contento (-a), (-os), (-as)
heavy	pesado (-a), (-os), (-as)
high	alto (-a), (-os), (-as)
hired	contratado (-a), (-os), (-as)
hot (water, food, etc.)	caliente, calientes
hot (weather)	hace calor
important	importante, importantes
little	pequeño (-a), (-os), (-as)
low	bajo (-a), (-os), (-as)
necessary	necesario (-a), (-os), (-as)
new	nuevo (-a), (-os), (-as)
old	viejo (-a), (-os), (-as) / antiguo (-a), (-os), (-as)
open	abierto (-a), (-os), (-as)
personal	personal, personales
punctual	puntual, puntuales
rubber	de hule / de goma
self-cleaning	automático (-a), (-os), (-as)
sick	enfermo (-a), (-os), (-as)
slippery	resbaloso (-a), (-os), (-as)
small	pequeño (-a), (-os), (-as)
strange	extraño (-a), (-os), (-as)
sturdy	fuerte, fuertes
sunny	hace sol
tepid	tibio (-a), (-os), (-as)
unlocked	abierto (-a), (-os), (-as)

128

unsupervised	sin vigilar
upholstered	tapizado (-a), (-os), (-as)
upright	parado (-a), (-os), (-as)
valuable	valioso (-a), (-os), (-as)
wet	mojado (-a), (-os), (-as)
white	blanco (-a), (-os), (-as)
whole	entero (-a), (-os), (-as)
windy	hace viento
wooden	de madera

Words That Tell *How*

by hand	a mano
carefully	con cuidado
fine (not sick)	bien
fine (weather)	buen tiempo
separately	por separado
slowly	lento
so-so	más o menos / regular
well	bien

Words That Tell *When*

advance, in	por adelantado
always	siempre / en todo momento
A.M.	de la mañana
at all times	en todo momento
early	temprano
every day	todos los días
late	tarde
later	más tarde
midnight	medianoche
never	nunca
noon	mediodía
now	ahora
on the dot	en punto
on time	puntual
P.M.	de la tarde / de la noche
promptly	cuanto antes
soon	pronto
today	hoy
until _____	hasta _____
while _____	mientras _____

Words That Tell *How Much* or *How Many*

a few	unos pocos, unas pocas
a little	un poco
little (amount)	poco
many	muchos
many times	muchas veces
one time	una vez
several	varios, varias
too many	demasiado (-a), (-os), (-as)
two times	dos veces

Words That Tell *Where*

at	en
behind	detrás de
between	entre
down there	abajo
downstairs	abajo
far	lejos
here	aquí
home (at)	en casa
home (toward)	a casa
in	en
in back of	detrás de
in front of	delante de
left (direction)	a la izquierda
near	cerca
next to	al lado de
on	en
on top of	encima de
out of	fuera de
outside	afuera
over there	allí
right (direction)	a la derecha
there	ahí
through	por
under	por debajo de
underneath	debajo de
up there	arriba
upstairs	arriba

Words That Tell *Whose*

her	su, sus
hers	suyo (-a), (-os), (-as)
his	su, sus / suyo (-a), (-os), (-as)
mine	mío (-a), (-os), (-as)
my	mi, mis
our, ours	nuestro (-a), (-os), (-as)
own (belonging to)	propio (-a), (-os), (-as)
theirs	suyo (-a), (-os), (-as)
your	su, sus
yours	suyo (-a), (-os), (-as)

Little Words

alone	solo
at	en
because	porque
before	antes
depending	depende
extra	extra
first	primero
first (most important)	primordial
if	si
like that	así
like this	así
maybe	quizás
per	por
that	ese, esa
these	estas, estos
this	este, esta
those	esas, esos
to	a
with	con
with me	conmigo
without	sin

Activities

Note: In this section, the words for activities are given in their *infinitive* form, the basic dictionary form, which does *not* indicate who is doing the action. In the text of the book, most of the "action words" are given in the command form, appropriate for giving instructions.

accept	aceptar
add	añadir
advise (tell)	avisar
answer	contestar
arrive	llegar
ask	preguntar
ask for	pedir
bathe	bañar
be	estar
begin	empezar
behave	portarse bien
break	romper
bring	traer
burp / make burp	eructar / hacer eructar
button	abotonar
buy	comprar
call	llamar
calm	calmar / tranquilizar
can (be able to)	poder
change	cambiar
clean	limpiar
clear (table)	retirar los platos
close	cerrar
comb	peinar
come	venir
come in	entrar
contact	contactar
cook	cocinar
cross	cruzar
cry	llorar
disconnect	desenchufar
do (make)	hacer
dress	vestir
drop	dejar caer
dry	secar
dust	pasar el trapo
eat	comer
empty	vaciar
expect	esperar
fall	caer
feed	dar de comer a

English-Spanish Glossary

fill	llenar
finish	terminar
fire (from a job)	despedir
firm, be	mantenerse firme
fold	doblar
follow	seguir
frighten	espantar
get along with	llevarse bien con
get cold	enfriarse
go out	salir
hang up	colgar
have	tener
heat	calentar
help	ayudar
hire	contratar
hold the hand of	agarrar la mano de
iron (clothing)	planchar
keep	guardar / mantener
keep away	mantener lejos
knock	tocar
lay (place)	colocar
leave (go out)	salir
leave (let stay)	dejar
let	dejar
let cool	dejar enfriar
listen	escuchar
live	vivir
lock	cerrar con llave
make	hacer
make the bed	arreglar la cama
may	poder
maybe	quizás
measure	medir
misbehave	portarse mal
mix	mezclar
mop	pasar el trapeador
move (things)	mover
move (to a new house)	mudarse
must	deber
need	necesitar
open	abrir
operate	operar
park (a car)	estacionarse
pay	pagar
pick up	recoger

English-Spanish Glossary

place (put down)	colocar
play	jugar
plug in	enchufar
polish	lustrar / sacarle brillo
polish (furniture)	limpiar con cera
polish (silver)	limpiar la plata
provide	proporcionar
pull	jalar
punish	castigar
push	empujar
push (button)	apretar
put	poner
put away	poner en su lugar
put on	poner
put to bed	acostar
rain	llover
raise	aumentar
reach	alcanzar
read	leer
remove (take off)	quitar
remove (take out)	sacar
rest	descansar
return	volver
rinse	enjuagar
rock (a baby)	acunar en la mecedora
run (machine)	funcionar
scrub	fregar
send	enviar
separate	separar
set the table	poner la mesa
shower	ducharse
smoke	fumar
snow	nevar
spank	pegar
spot-clean	limpiar las manchas
spray	usar el espray
sprinkle	salpicar
start (machine)	poner en marcha
stay	quedarse
straighten	arreglar
sweep	barrer
take	llevar
take out	sacar
talk	hablar
tell	decir

English-Spanish Glossary

threaten	amenazar
throw away	tirar / echar
tie (up)	atar
touch	tocar
treat	tratar
turn off (machine, light)	apagar
turn off (water)	cerrar la llave del agua
turn on (machine, light)	encender
turn on (water)	abrir la llave del agua
turn the dial	girar el indicador
understand	entender
undress	desvestir
unplug	desenchufar
use	usar
vacuum	pasar la aspiradora
wait	esperar
wash	lavar
watch (children)	vigilar
watch (television, game)	ver
wipe	pasarle un trapo
wipe off	quitar
work (function)	funcionar
work (labor)	trabajar
wrap	envolver
yell at	gritar a

Things

activity	actividad
affection	cariño
alarm system	sistema de seguridad
ammonia	amoníaco
animal	animal
animals (pets)	mascotas
animals, strange	animales desconocidos
ants	hormigas
anything	cualquier cosa
appliances	aparatos
armchair	sillón
ashtray	cenicero
attic	desván
attitude	actitud
baby carriage	cochecito
baseboards	zócalos

135

English-Spanish Glossary

bath mat	tapete
bathtub	bañera / tina
bed	cama
bedspread	sobrecama
belt	cinturón
blankets	cobijas / mantas / frazadas
bleach	lejía
blender	batidora
blinds	persianas
blouse	blusa
bones	huesos
books	libros
bookshelves	estantes
bottle (for baby)	biberón
box	caja
box, jewelry	joyero
braids	trenzas
break (rest)	descanso
breakfast	desayuno
broiler	asador
broom	escoba
brush	cepillo
bucket	cubeta
buffet	aparador
bugs	bichos
burners	quemadores
button	botón
cabinet, china	vitrina
cabinet, filing	archivador
cabinet, television	mueble del televisor
can	lata
candlesticks	candelabros
candy	dulces
canister	lata
carpet	alfombra
carpet cleaner	limpiador de alfombras
carriage, baby	cochecito
cash	efectivo
cat	gato
ceiling fan	ventilador
chair	silla
chair, easy	sillón
check	cheque
chemicals	químicas
chest of drawers	cómoda

china	vajilla
china cabinet	vitrina
chlorine bleach	cloro
chores	tareas
cleaner, carpet	limpiador de alfombras
cleaner, floor	limpiador de suelos
cleaner, spray	limpiador espray
cleaning supplies	limpiadores / productos para la limpieza
clock	reloj
closet	guardarropa
cloth	trapo
clothes	ropa
clothes, dirty	ropa sucia
clothing	ropa
clothing, dark	ropa oscura
clothing, light	ropa blanca
cobweb	telaraña
coffee	café
computer	computadora
computer screen	pantalla
copier	fotocopiadora
corner (inside)	rincón
corner (outside)	esquina
counter (bathroom)	tocador
countertop	mostrador
crib	cuna
crystal	cristal fino
cupboard	gabinete
curtain	cortina
curtain rod	barra para la cortina
cycle, wash	programa de lavado
date	fecha
day	día
decoration	ornamento
decorative objects	objetos decorativos
desk	escritorio
detergent	detergente
dial	indicador
diaper	pañal
dinner	cena
directions	instrucciones
dirt	suciedad
dishes	platos
dishwasher	lavaplatos

137

documents	documentos
dog	perro
door	puerta
doorbell	timbre
drain	desagüe
drawer	cajón
dress	vestido
dresser	tocador
drink	refresco / algo de beber
driveway	entrada
dry mop	trapeador seco
dryer	secadora
dust	polvo
duster	plumero
dustpan	pala
easy chair	sillón
eggshells	cáscaras de los huevos
electronic equipment	equipo electrónico
emergency	emergencia
equipment	aparatos
experience	experiencia
fabric softener	suavizante de telas
face	cara
fan	ventilador
faucet	llave del agua
fax machine	fax
filing cabinet	archivador
filter	filtro
fingerprints	huellas
fireplace	chimenea
fireplace equipment	herramientas para la chimenea
floor	suelo
floor polisher	enceradora de suelos
flowers	flores
flowers, dead	flores muertas
food	comida / alimentos
food processor	procesador de alimentos
footstool	taburete
fork	tenedor
freezer	congelador
frying pan	sartén
furniture	muebles
furniture (upholstered)	muebles tapizados
furniture polish	cera para muebles
garbage disposer	triturador

English-Spanish Glossary

gift	regalo
glass (drinking)	vaso
glass	vidrio
glasses (for vision)	anteojos
gloves	guantes
grill	parrilla
hair	pelo
hamper	canasta
hand	mano
handbag	cartera
hard substances	elementos duras
health	salud
heat / heater	calefacción
help	ayuda
hood (stove)	campana extractora
hour	hora
house	casa
income	ingresos
insecticide	insecticida
insects	insectos
instructions	instrucciones
iron (clothes)	plancha
ironing board	burro de planchar
it	lo, la
item	cosa
jacket	chaqueta
jewelry box	joyero
job	trabajo
juice	jugo
key	llave
keyboard	teclado
knife	cuchillo
lamp	lámpara
lampshade	pantalla
laptop	computadora portátil
level	nivel
lid	tapa
light	luz
light fixture	lámpara
linen	ropa blanca
lint filter	filtro
lock	cerradura
lunch	almuerzo
machine	máquina
magazine	revista

mark (stain)	mancha
mat, bath	tapete
medicine	medicina
message	mensaje
metal	metal
mice	ratones
microwave	microondas
milk	leche
minute	minuto
mirror	espejo
mixer	batidor
moment	momento
month	mes
mop	trapeador
mop, dry	trapeador seco
mop, wet	trapeador mojado
mouse	ratón
name	nombre
necktie	corbata
night table	mesa de noche
noise	ruido
number	número
nuts	nueces
objects, small	objetos pequeños
ornament	ornamento
outfit	conjunto
oven	horno
painting	pintura
pajamas	piyama
pants	pantalón, pantalones
paper	papel
pasta	pasta
payment	pago
peelings	peladuras
pen	pluma / lapicero
pencil	lápiz
pests	animales indeseables
photograph	fotografía
piano	piano
picture (painting)	pintura
picture (photograph)	fotografía
picture (on wall)	cuadro
pillowcases	fundas
planter	maceta
plastic	plástico

plug (electric)	enchufe
pocketbook	cartera
polish, floor	enceradora de suelos
polish, furniture	cera para muebles
ponytail	cola de caballo
photographs	fotografías
pots and pans	trastes
printer	impresora
problem	problema
product	producto
purse	cartera
radio	radio
rag	trapo
raise	aumento
rats	ratas
reference	referencia
refrigerator	nevera / refrigeradora
rice	arroz
rug	alfombra
safety	seguridad
salary	sueldo
scale	balanza
scissors	tijeras
Scotch tape	cinta
screen, computer	pantalla
screen, television	pantalla
screen, window	tela metálica de la ventana
seeds	semillas
serving cart	mesa rodante
shampoo	champú
sheets	sábanas
shelf (individual)	repisa
shelves (set of)	estante
shirt	camisa
shoes	zapatos
shower	ducha
shower curtain	cortina de la ducha
shredder	trituradora
sidewalk	acera
silverware	cubiertos
sink (bathroom)	lavabo
sink (kitchen)	fregadero
size	tamaño
size (clothing)	talla
size (shoes)	número

skills	habilidades
skirt	falda
smoke	humo
snack	antojito
snake	culebra
snow	nieve
soap	jabón
soap dish	jabonera
Social Security	Seguridad Social
socks	calcetines
sofa	sofá
soft drinks	refrescos
softener, fabric	suavizante de telas
spiders	arañas
sponge	esponja
spoon	cuchara
spot	mancha
spray	espray
spray cleaner	limpiador espray
stapler	grapadora
stockings	medias
storm	tormenta
stove	estufa
street	calle
stroller (child's)	sillita
study	estudio
subway	metro
suit	traje
supplies, office	artículos de la oficina
surface	superficie
sweater	suéter
table	mesa
table, night	mesa de noche
tablecloth	mantel
tape, Scotch	cinta
taxes	impuestos
tea	té
telephone	teléfono
television (program)	televisión
television (set)	televisor
television cabinet	mueble del televisor
temperature	temperatura
thing	cosa
tile	azulejo
time (hour)	hora

English-Spanish Glossary

time (period)	tiempo
timer	reloj
toaster	tostador
toilet	inodoro
toothpicks	palillos
top (lid)	tapa
towel	toalla
toys	juguetes
train	tren
trap	trampa
trash	basura
trashcan	basurero
underwear	ropa interior
utensils	utensilios
vacuum cleaner	aspiradora
vase	florero
vent	escape
vinegar	vinagre
volume	volumen
wages	sueldo
wall	pared
wardrobe	armario
wash cycle	programa de lavado
washing machine	lavadora
wastebasket	canasta / cesta de la basura
water	agua
wax	cera
weather	tiempo
week	semana
weekend	fin de semana
wet mop	trapeador mojado
Windex	Windex
window	ventana
windowsill	repisa
wood	madera
work	trabajo

Glosario español-inglés

Expresiones

¿Adónde... ?	Where to . . . ?
¿Cómo... ?	How . . . ?
¿Cómo está usted?	How are you?
¿Cómo se dice... ?	How do you say . . . ?
¿Con quién... ?	With whom . . . ?
¿Cuál... ?	What . . . ?
¿Cuándo... ?	When . . . ?
¿Cuánto... ?	How much . . . ?
¿Cuántos... ?	How many . . . ?
¿De dónde... ?	From where . . . ?
¿De quién... ?	Whose . . . ?
¿Dónde... ?	Where . . . ?
¿Hasta cuándo... ?	Until when . . . ?
¡Ojalá!	God willing!
¿Para qué... ?	What for . . . ?
¿Por cuánto tiempo... ?	For how long . . . ?
¿Por qué?	Why . . . ?
¿Qué... ?	What . . . ?
¿Quién... ?	Who . . . ?

Expresiones prácticas y de cortesía

Adiós.	Good-bye.
Bienvenido.	Welcome.
Buenas noches.	Good night.
Buenas tardes. / noches.	Good evening.
Buenas tardes.	Good afternoon.
Buenos días.	Good morning.

Glosario español-inglés

Cuidado. / Tenga cuidado.	Be careful.
de la mañana	A.M.
de la tarde / de la noche	P.M.
De nada.	You're welcome.
Disculpe.	Excuse me.
Gracias.	Thank you.
Hasta luego.	See you later.
Hola.	Hello.
Llame al nueve-uno-uno.	Call 911.
Lo siento.	I'm sorry.
No...	Don't . . .
No.	No.
Por favor.	Please.
Sí.	Yes.

Personas

alguien	someone
amigo, amiga	friend
bebé	baby
él	he
ella	she
ellos / ellas	they
esposa	wife
esposo	husband
hermana	sister
hermano	brother
hija	daughter
hijo	son
hijos, hijas	children (sons and daughters)
jefe, jefa	boss
la / le / a ella	her
lo / le / a él	him
madre	mother
niñera	babysitter
niño, niña	child
niños, niñas	children
nosotros, nosotras	we
novia	girlfriend
novio	boyfriend
padre	father
padres	parents
patrón, patrona	boss
persona desconocida	stranger

usted	you
ustedes	you (all)
vecino, vecina	neighbor
yo	I

Lugares

baño	bathroom
biblioteca	library
cocina	kitchen
comedor	dining room
cuarto	bedroom
cuarto de los niños	nursery
cuarto de recreo	playroom
despacho	office
despensa	pantry
dormitorio	bedroom
garaje	garage
habitación	room
lavandería	laundry room / utility room
lugar	place
oficina	office
parada de autobuses	bus stop
parque	park
pasillo	hall
patio	patio
porche	porch
recámara	bedroom
sala	living room
sala familiar	family room
sótano	basement

Palabras que describen a personas, lugares o cosas

abierto	open / unlocked
acostado	flat (position)
alto	high
antiguo	very old / antique
automático	automatic
bajo	low
blanco	white
bueno	good

Glosario español-inglés

caliente	hot
calor (hace calor)	it's hot (in here; outside)
contento	happy
contratado	hired
despedido	fired (from a job)
enfermo	sick
entero	whole
extraño	strange
frágil	fragile
frío	cold
fuerte	sturdy
goma, de	rubber
grande	big
hule, de	rubber
húmedo	damp
importante	important
limpio	clean
madera, de	wooden
malo	bad
mojado	wet
muerto	dead
necesario	necessary
nublado	cloudy
nuevo	new
oscuro	dark
parado	upright
peligroso	dangerous
pequeño	little / small
personal	personal
pesado	heavy
puntual	punctual
resbaloso	slippery
roto	broken
seco	dry
soleado	sunny
sucio	dirty
tapizado	upholstered
templado	cool
tibio	tepid
tranquilo	calm
vacío	empty
valioso	valuable
viejo	old
viento, hace	windy
vigilar, sin	unsupervised

Palabras que indican *cómo*

a mano	by hand
bien	fine / well
buen tiempo	fine (weather)
cuidadosamente	carefully
lento	slowly
más o menos	so-so
separado, por	separately

Palabras que indican *cuándo*

adelantado, por	in advance
ahora	now
cuanto antes	promptly / right away
en punto	on the dot
hasta _____	until _____
hoy	today
más tarde	later
medianoche, a	at midnight
mediodía, a	at noon / at midday
mientras _____	while _____
nunca	never
pronto	soon
puntual	on time
siempre	always
temprano	early
todos los días	every day

Palabras que indican *cuánto* o *cuántos*

demasiado	too many / too much
dos veces	two times
muchas veces	many times
muchos	many
poco	little (amount)
un poco	a little
una vez	one time
unos pocos	a few
varios	several

Palabras que indican *dónde*

a casa (toward)	home
a la derecha	right (direction)
a la izquierda	left (direction)
abajo	down there / downstairs
afuera	outside
ahí	there
al lado de	next to
allí	over there
aquí	here
arriba	up there / upstairs
cerca	near
debajo de	underneath
delante de	in front of
dentro (de)	inside
detrás de	in back of / behind
en	in / on / at
en casa	at home
encima de	on top of
entre	between
fuera de	out of
lejos	far
por	through
por debajo de	under

Palabras que indican *de quién*

mi, mis	my
mío	mine
nuestro	our, ours
propio	one's own
su, sus	your / his / her / their
suyo	yours / his / hers / theirs

Palabras pequeñas

a	to
antes	before
así	like this / like that
con	with
conmigo	with me

depende	depending
en	in / on / at
esas, esos	those
ese, esa	that
estas, estos	these
este, esta	this
extra	extra
por	per / through
porque	because
primero	first
primordial	most important
quizás	maybe
si	if
sin	without
solo	alone

Actividades

abotonar	button
abrir	open
abrir la llave	turn on (water)
aceptar	accept
acostar	put to bed
acunar en la mecedora	rock (a baby)
agarrar la mano de	hold the hand of
alcanzar	reach
amenazar	threaten
añadir	add
apagar	turn off (machine, light)
apretar	push (button)
arreglar	straighten
arreglar la cama	make the bed
atar	tie (up)
aumentar	raise
avisar	advise (tell)
ayudar	help
bañar	bathe
barrer	sweep
caer	fall
calentar	heat
calmar	calm down
cambiar	change
castigar	punish
cerrar	close

Glosario español-inglés

cerrar	turn off (water)
cerrar con llave	lock
cocinar	cook
colgar	hang up
colocar	lay / place
comer	eat
comprar	buy
contactar	contact
contestar	answer
contratar	hire
cruzar	cross
dar de comer a	feed
deber	must
decir	tell
dejar	leave / let
dejar caer	drop
dejar enfriar	let cool
descansar	rest
desenchufar	disconnect / unplug
despedir	fire
desvestir	undress
doblar	fold
ducharse	shower
echar	throw out
empezar	begin
empujar	push
encender	turn on (machine, light)
enchufar	plug in
enfriarse	get cold
enjuagar	rinse
entender	understand
entrar	come in
enviar	send
envolver	wrap
eructar / hacer eructar	burp / make burp
escuchar	listen
espantar	frighten
esperar	expect / wait
estacionarse	park
estar	be
fregar	scrub
fumar	smoke
funcionar	run / work (machine)
girar el indicador	turn the dial
gritar a	yell at

Glosario español-inglés

guardar	keep
hablar	talk
hacer	do / make
jalar	pull
jugar	play
lavar	wash
leer	read
limpiar	clean
limpiar con cera	polish (furniture)
limpiar la plata	polish the silver
limpiar las manchas	spot-clean
llamar	call
llegar	arrive
llenar	fill
llevar	take
llevarse bien con	get along with
llorar	cry
llover	rain
lustrar	polish
mantener	keep
mantener lejos	keep away
mantenerse firme	be firm
medir	measure
mezclar	mix
mover	move (things)
mudarse	move to a new house
necesitar	need
nevar	snow
operar	operate
pagar	pay
pasar el trapeador	mop
pasar el trapo	dust / wipe
pasar la aspiradora	vacuum
pedir	ask for
pegar	spank / hit
peinar	comb
planchar	iron (clothing)
poder	can / be able to / may
poner	put
poner en marcha	start (machine)
poner en su lugar	put away
poner la mesa	set the table
portarse bien	behave
portarse mal	misbehave
preguntar	ask

proporcionar	provide
quedarse	stay
quitar	remove / take off / wipe off
recoger	pick up
retirar los platos	clear the table
romper	break
sacar	remove / take out
sacarle brillo	polish
salir	leave / go out
salpicar	sprinkle
secar	dry
seguir	follow
separar	separate
tener	have
terminar	finish
tirar	throw out
tocar	knock / touch
trabajar	work (to labor)
traer	bring
tranquilizar	calm down
tratar	treat
usar	use
usar el espray	spray
vaciar	empty
venir	come
ver	watch (television, game)
vestir	dress
vigilar	watch (children)
vivir	live
volver	return

Cosas

acera	sidewalk
actitud	attitude
actividad	activity
agua	water
alfombra	rug / carpet
almuerzo	lunch
amoníaco	ammonia
animal	animal
animales desconocidos	strange animals
animales indeseables	pests
anteojos	eyeglasses

Glosario español-inglés

antojito	snack
aparador	buffet
aparatos	appliances / equipment
arañas	spiders
archivador	filing cabinet
armario	storage closet / cupboard
armario para ropa blanca	linen closet
arroz	rice
artículos de la oficina	office supplies
asador	broiler
aspiradora	vacuum cleaner
aumento	raise
ayuda	help
azulejo	wall tile
balanza	scale
bañera	bathtub
barra para la cortina	curtain rod
basura	trash
basurero	trash can
batidor	mixer
batidora	blender
biberón	baby bottle
bichos	bugs
blusa	blouse
botón	button
burro de planchar	ironing board
café	coffee
caja	box
cajón	drawer
calcetines	socks
calefacción	heat / heater
calle	street
cama	bed
camisa	shirt
campana extractora	hood (stove)
canasta	hamper / basket
canasta de la basura	wastebasket
candelabros	candlesticks
cara	face
cariño	affection
carro	car
cartera	handbag / pocketbook / purse / wallet
casa	house
cáscaras de los huevos	eggshells
cena	dinner

Glosario español-inglés

cenicero	ashtray
cepillo	brush
cera	wax
cera para muebles	furniture polish
cerradura	lock
cesta de la basura	wastepaper basket
champú	shampoo
chaqueta	jacket
cheque	check
chimenea	fireplace
cinta	Scotch tape
cinturón	belt
cloro	chlorine bleach
cobijas	blankets
cochecito	baby carriage
cola de caballo	ponytail
comida liviana	snacks
cómoda	chest of drawers
computadora	computer
computadora portátil	laptop
congelador	freezer
conjunto	outfit
corbata	necktie
cortina	curtain
cortina de la ducha	shower curtain
cosa	thing / item
cristal fino	crystal
cuadro	picture (on wall)
cualquier cosa	anything
cubeta	bucket
cubiertos	silverware
cuchara	spoon
cuchillo	knife
culebra	snake
cuna	crib
desagüe	drain
desayuno	breakfast
descanso	break (rest)
desván	attic
detergente	detergent
día	day
documentos	documents
ducha	shower
dulces	candy
efectivo	cash

emergencia	emergency
enceradora de suelos	floor polish / floor polisher
enchufe	plug (electric)
entrada	entrance / driveway
equipo electrónico	electronic equipment
escape	vent
escoba	broom
escritorio	desk
espejo	mirror
esponja	sponge
espray	spray
esquina	corner (outside)
estante	(set of) shelves
estudio	study
estufa	stove
experiencia	experience
falda	skirt
fax	fax machine
fecha	date
filtro	filter
fin de semana	weekend
florero	vase
flores	flowers
flores muertas	dead flowers
fotocopiadora	copier
fotografía (foto)	photograph
fregadero	kitchen sink
fundas	pillowcases
gabinete	cupboard
gato	cat
grapadora	stapler
guantes	gloves
guardarropa	clothes closet
habilidades	skills
herramientas para la chimenea	fireplace equipment
hora	time (hour)
hormigas	ants
horno	oven
huellas	fingerprints
huesos	bones
humo	smoke
impresora	printer (computer)
impuestos	taxes
indicador	dial
ingresos	income

Glosario español-inglés

inodoro	toilet
insecticida	insecticide
insectos	insects
instrucciones	instructions
jabón	soap
jabonera	soap dish
joyero	jewelry box
jugo	juice
juguetes	toys
lámpara	lamp / light fixture
lapicero	pen
lápiz	pencil
lata	can / canister
lavabo	bathroom sink
lavadora	washing machine
lavaplatos	dishwasher
leche	milk
lejía	bleach
libros	books
limpiador de alfombras	carpet cleaner
limpiador de suelos	floor cleaner
limpiador espray	spray cleaner
limpiadores	cleaning supplies
llave	key
llave del agua	faucet
lo, la	it
luz	light
maceta	planter
madera	wood
mancha	mark / spot
mano	hand
mantel	tablecloth
máquina	machine
mascotas	pets
materiales duros	hard substances
medias	stockings
medicina	medicine
mensaje	message
mes	month
mesa	table
mesa de noche	night table
mesa rodante	serving cart
metal	metal
metro	subway
microondas	microwave

minute	minuto
momento	moment
mostrador	countertop
mueble del televisor	television cabinet
muebles	furniture
muebles tapizados	upholstered furniture
nevera	refrigerator
nieve	snow
nivel	level
nombre	name
nueces	nuts
número	number / shoe size
objetos decorativos	decorative objects
ornamento	decoration / ornament
pago	payment
pala	dustpan
palillos	toothpicks
pañal	diaper
pantalla	computer screen / television screen / lampshade
pantalón, pantalones	pants
papel	paper
pared	wall
parrilla	grill
pasta	pasta
peladuras	peelings
pelo	hair
perro	dog
persianas	blinds
piano	piano
pintura	painting
piyama	pajamas
plancha	clothes iron
plástico	plastic
platos	dishes
pluma	pen / feather
plumero	duster
polvo	dust
problema	problem
procesador de alimentos	food processor
producto	product
productos para la limpieza	cleaning supplies
programa de lavado	washing cycle
puerta	door
quemadores	stove burners

químicas	chemicals
radio	radio
ratas	rats
ratones	mice
referencia	reference
refresco	drink
refrigeradora	refrigerator
regalo	gift
reloj	clock / timer
repisa	shelf / windowsill
revista	magazine
rincón	corner (inside)
ropa	clothes / clothing
ropa blanca	light-colored clothes (laundry) / bed linen and towels
ropa interior	underwear
ropa oscura	dark-colored clothes (laundry)
ropa sucia	dirty clothes
ruido	noise
sábanas	sheets
salud	health
sartén	frying pan
secadora	dryer
seguridad	safety
Seguridad Social	Social Security
semana	week
semillas	seeds
silla	chair
sillita	stroller
sillón	armchair / easy chair
sistema de seguridad	alarm system
sobrecama	bedspread
sofá	sofa
suavizante de telas	fabric softener
suciedad	dirt
sueldo	salary / wages
suelo	floor
suéter	sweater
superficie	surface
taburete	footstool
talla	size (clothing)
tamaño	size
tapa	lid
tapete	bath mat
tareas	chores / homework

159

Glosario español-inglés

té	tea
teclado	keyboard
tela metálica de la ventana	screen (window)
telaraña	cobweb
teléfono	telephone
televisión	television (program)
televisor	television set
temperatura	temperature
tenedor	fork
tiempo	time (period) / weather
tina	bathtub
tijeras	scissors
timbre	doorbell
toalla	towel
tocador	counter (bathroom) / dresser / chest of drawers
top (lid)	tapa
tormenta	storm
tostador	toaster
trabajo	job / work
traje	suit
trampa	trap
trapeador	mop
trapeador mojado	wet mop
trapeador seco	dry mop
trapo	cloth / rag
trastes	pots and pans
tren	train
trenzas	braids
triturador	garbage disposer
trituradora	shredder
utensilios	utensils
vajilla	china
vaso	glass (drinking)
ventana	window
ventilador	fan
vestido	dress
vidrio	glass
vinagre	vinegar
vitrina	china cabinet
volumen	volume
zapatos	shoes
zócalos	baseboards